In
the Company
of Cowboys

Author
Howard E Greager

In
the Company
of Cowboys

Howard E. Greager

To my daughter, Rebecca L. Curtis—in grateful appreciation of all the wonderful help and for putting the spark to the "old plug" to get this volume to the press

CONTENTS

ACKNOWLEDGMENTS

I would like to take this opportunity to publicly thank just a few of the lovely people who gave so generously of their time to help make this book a reality:

Dewey and Essie Greager (my parents)—*deceased*
Mr. Fred Sharp (a great cowboy and storyteller)—*deceased*
The Outlaw Ed Williams (for his contribution to the old west)—*deceased*
Mr. Earnest Maupin (for a wealth of cowboy lore; died at 103)—*deceased*
Mr. Earnest Andress—*deceased*
Mrs. Hazel Garner—*Grand Junction, Colorado*
Mrs. Jane Royer—*Norwood, Colorado*
Mr. William E. Bray—*Redvale, Colorado*
Mr. Al Williams—*Norwood, Colorado*
Mr. Wilson Rockwell—*Creston, British Columbia*
Mr. Stanley Reed—*deceased*
Mr. Vernon W. Bankston (classmate of 1942 and lifelong friend)—*deceased*
Wilma Crisp Bankston (author of the book *Where Eagles Winter*)—*Cortez, Colorado*
Mr. Jesse West—*Shiprock, New Mexico*
Josephine Patten—*Grand Junction, Colorado*
W. R. Doherty (artist)—*Delta, Colorado*
Mr. Al Scorup—*Grand Junction, Colorado*
Keith A. Greager (a tremendous help indeed: Thanks)—*Dove Creek, Colorado*
Colorado Historical Society—*Denver, Colorado*

Naturita Historical Museum—*Naturita, Colorado*
The San Miguel Basin State Bank—*Norwood, Colorado*
The Montrose *Daily Press*—*Montrose, Colorado*
The Grand Junction *Daily Sentinel*—*Grand Junction, Colorado*
Mr. Frank Calhoun—*Deceased*
Museum of Western Colorado—*Grand Junction, Colorado*

ABOUT THE ARTIST

W. R. "Dick" Doherty grew up in New York City before moving as a young man into agricultural work upstate. Drifting around the country he worked at different jobs, and in the early fifties moved west to learn to be a cowboy. He spent several years as a cowhand in Wyoming, North Dakota, and Colorado. His natural love of outdoor life, working cattle, hunting, camping, and the beauty of nature became a part of his experience and expression.

Art has been a part of Dick's life since he began drawing at the age of four. He was fifteen before he discovered his skill in oil painting and his love for this medium continues to this day. Throughout his travels Dick drew and painted, recording the life he loves from the interplay of his experience, memories, and imagination.

Wherever he went his ability was soon recognized and people frequently called on him to use his artwork in various ways. It wasn't until he was in his thirties that the idea of developing his talent into a way of life became real for him. In Norwood, Colorado, the community saw Dick as the answer to their need for an art teacher in their school. Community support and Dick's decision to answer the school's request led to his new career as an artist and art teacher rather than an artist and cowboy.

Dick has since earned a bachelor and a masters degree in Fine Arts, taught art in public high school, college, and community adult classes and workshops. Throughout his teaching years, he has pursued his own creative career through public and private commissions, shows, and sales. He works in a variety of media including pen and ink, oil, water color, pastel, and printmaking. Some special projects he designed include a bicentennial monument, commemorative coin, a sixteen foot by seventy foot wildlife mural for Delta, Colorado and a book of pen and ink drawings of landmarks of the San Miguel Basin.

Realistic representations of western life, wildlife, and scenery are the meat of his work. He presents his ideas of things as he sees and remembers them, relying on the inherent beauty and interest of his subjects to speak for themselves without being romanticized or exaggerated.

Dick is now a full-time artist and is exploring the range of material his rich experience, clear perceptions, and love of western life present.

INTRODUCTION

If the late western author Louis L'Amour had been looking for an authentic westerner—one with the heart of an old-time cowhand, the passion of a displaced rancher, and the political indignation of a Mark Twain—he could have sat down awhile with Norwood's Howard Greager, who's well-known as a local author and raconteur.

Until publishing *In the Company of Cowboys*, sixty-five year-old Greager was most often read in the area's newspapers. He has written most recently about the subject of wild horses ("They've been under trespass to Bureau Land Management [BLM] since 1948. . . . "). Prior to that, Greager produced a lengthy and authoritative public account about a late season special elk hunt.

Tall and lean enough to have been Gary Cooper's stand-in, Greager looks the part of a well-seasoned rancher, and is recognized by most San Miguel area ranchers as a top hand with horses. Although Howard inherited his Dad's horsemanship and, perhaps, a bit of his luck, neither man was able to make ranching his livelihood. Despite his ranching heritage and natural abilities, Greager spent most of his working life making a living off the range. In fact, he says he's been everything from a bartender to a barber, figures he's held thirty-three different jobs, and has a resume "that appalled one prospective employer."

Since mining, welding, mechanics, and other trades paid better, and Greager had a growing family of his own, he gave up the idea of ranching as a full-time occupation. In recent years Greager's job history has been a profile of the region's economics. Starting in 1966, he worked in Telluride as an Idarado Mining Company maintenance mechanic until the mine and mill shut down in 1978. From there, he accepted similar work at Union Carbide's famous Sunday Mine, in western San Miguel County's Gypsum Valley. Along with many laborers in the uranium industry, Greager was out of a job again when the Sunday closed down in 1983. The following late summer, he worked for Umetco Minerals Company (formerly Union Carbide) at its Uravan mill until that operation was again shut down after a three-month run. "The country's changing," Greager says with a certain resignation.

Still, he managed to keep his hand in "the ranch life" over the last thirty-five years by shoeing horses for friends. He earned the reputation with San Miguel ranchers as the best in the region. Although he is pretty much retired now, Greager still enjoys teaching his trade secrets to young horseshoeing students.

"I always had a good way with horses. We talked the same language," Greager says with a touch of pride. He admits to becoming "quite proficient" shoeing horses that nobody else could handle, and claims, "I never lost my temper. I've seen a few horses that'd almost eat you alive." He also says he's been bitten, kicked, knocked down, tromped on and ripped apart in a few places by flying feet bristling with unbent horseshoe nails.

Most of the twenty stories Greager has compiled for his book came originally from storytelling sessions with the region's premier storyteller, Fred Sharp, who is also one of the central characters in the book. Tough and colorful, Fred Sharp was a small, slight man but a superb cowboy. As young men, Sharp and the author's father, "Dewey" Greager, began making their living in 1902 by catching unbranded cattle, descendants of Mexican strays running wild on the open range. For four years the pair kept providing a steady supply of beef to Telluride's meat house and the tables of that thriving mining town. Howard Greager says that Sharp, a recognized expert at catching wild cattle, used a pair of Airedale dogs along with barriers and traps to snag the wily critters.

Fresh out of the U.S. Navy in 1946, Howard was a willing and temporarily available audience for storyteller Sharp. By then, Sharp was about seventy, badly crippled and on crutches, but still "a tough old rooster" and "absolutely the best storyteller. He never missed a date or a name and could tell some pretty fair history if you had time to listen," states Greager.

Material for other stories came directly from personal experiences, such as breaking the "Strawberry Roan" and hunting for his brothers in "Three Against the Storm." Greager learned about Disappointment Valley and the Spring Creek Basin's wild horse bunch early on. "When I was in high school, it was the greatest thing in the world to chase wild horses," says the author who often spent weekends with his classmate and best friend, the late Vernon Bankston, a Disappointment Valley rancher's son.

Rudolph "Dewey" Greager, a colorful old-timer himself, whose childhood reads like a Dickens novel of the American frontier, ran a Placerville saloon before his second marriage in 1916 and lost his entire Beaver Mesa cattle ranching operation during the 1929 stock market crash (a time when many of San Miguel's biggest operators "went down"). Some years later he was also the proprietor of Norwood's pool hall—a required fixture for any outpost west of the next place.

"Dewey," as he was universally known, won his nickname in 1898 when, as a young man, he was breaking cavalry horses for pioneer Placerville rancher, Bert Albin. Aspiring young cowboys learned their trade early, usually under the wing of a skilled older hand, and it was Albin "who made a horseman out of Dad," son Howard explains. Bert likened Rudy Greager's skill with horses to Admiral Dewey's naval victory during the Spanish American War—the big news of the day.

Among the many cowboys, miners, gamblers, and itiner-

xv

ants who frequented "Dewey" Greager's establishment during the 1930s was the legendary Ed Williams, a sort of low rent Robin Hood whose antics are firmly woven into San Miguel folklore. "Williams," says Howard Greager, "would often show up at the Greager residence after a heavy evening on the town. The house was a straight shot down main street to the west, and he hardly ever missed it. We would wake up in the night and find old Ed sitting on the edge of the bed. He would start telling stories about wild horses and wild cattle and a shootout with a sheriff." Greager claims Williams made a name for himself as a rough, tough cowboy known to have been in a few shooting scrapes. Charged by Disappointment Valley cattle ranchers with stealing their cattle, Williams made good on his promise to "shoot the rear end off any sheriff who tried to arrest him." Montrose Country Sheriff, H. C. Getty, suffered a terrible wound, but, due to prompt first aid by Williams and his common law wife, the sheriff was delivered to the doctors at Norwood in fairly stable condition.

In 1927, the law finally caught up with Williams, who did four years in the penitentiary. Today it's a mark of distinction to own a silver mounted bridle bit or pair of spurs turned out by Williams during his Canon City days. In later years, Williams, a big, well-built man, was easily recognized by his off-center gait and a crooked leg that was permanently turned outward as the result of a hastily misdirected rifle shot.

Once, the Disappointment Valley's wild horses meant pounding hooves and high excitement for two teenagers, but today the overgrown herd is another matter. Greager allows "there seems to be a lot of magic in the words 'wild horses'," and he wonders if sightseers drawn to visit the badlands just for a glimpse of the now fabled bunch "know what they're seeing?" He sides with the ranchers who pay to lease the Bureau of Land Management range where the unbranded wild horses eat free of charge. "I'm not advocating their destruction," he says of the trespassers.

Trespassing reminds him of another of the characters in his book, old Francis Hardman, a lower Disappointment Valley rancher who raised nothing but horses and sold them all over the country as "broke and ready to ride." During certain times of the year his horses were turned out to graze the BLM range illegally and occasionally would run off and join the wild bunch.

Today's wild horse herds of Spring Creek Basin are descendants of the horses Hardman and other hard-scrabble Disappointment Valley ranchers once turned out to graze free. Greager would like to see somebody take responsibility for managing today's herd and figures that that responsibility would include leasing the land and paying fees.

The storytelling gifts of the old-time cowboys may have come from a deep understanding of the part they had played in a great, real-life western epic. For Greager, the listener and the storyteller, there is a common theme to his collection of stories. From his interest in Fred Sharp's oral history of the region's early days to finding ways to deal fairly with today's Disappointment Valley wild horse herd, Greager's theme concerns people who live close to a land that only grudgingly produces a living but who make the most of it—on horseback, if possible.

—Grace Herndon
Norwood, Colorado
July 22, 1985

In
the Company
of Cowboys

Chapter 1

THE CHIPMUNK STEERS

While the San Juan Mountains were being opened up by the gold and silver miners in the late 1870s, the four towns of Telluride, Ouray, Silverton, and Rico were established. It seems that wherever there was a wide place in a river valley close in to the mines, a town would spring up—a place to construct buildings and dispense merchandise—a place with streets, and liveries, and saloons. Most of the mining towns started out in this fashion.

The quadrangle of the mining towns of Rico, Telluride, Ouray, and Silverton sprang up pretty much in the same two or three year span. The effort to supply these mountain towns with the necessary provisions would have been next to impossible without the use of the versatile and rugged burro and mule pack trains. Considered to be the backbone of any pack string, the handlers of these animals were called "skinners." The skills of knowing how to load, balance, and lash down were the tricks of the trade. The laborious, wearisome task of making their way through the rugged mountain terrain tested the men's skill, strength, and fortitude. For along the way, the "skinners" had to carve out their own trails into the mining towns once they had left the point where the ox teams and wagons could no longer go forward.

The quickest and easiest route into the mining towns was the goal of the trailbuilding "skinners" because many times the pack trains would often be loaded up with fresh beef quarters for the meat-starved miners of these regions. In time, slaughter-houses would be built within a few miles of the towns. Then, utilizing the trails built by the earlier "skinners," the cattle would be driven straight into the towns. For the first few years though, the pack stings carried the beef all the way from the slaughterhouses near Durango, Colorado.

In the period of time when the mining towns were spring-ing up in rugged Southwestern Colorado and the efforts to supply them were being coordinated, a man by the name of Alex Calhoun quickly became well-known. He was very soon re-garded as the best supplier not only for beef but also for just about all of the provisions that were needed by the mining towns. With a partner from Durango, Calhoun ran a large herd of cattle on what was then called the Blue Mountain Range. This range extended from the Blue Mountains in Utah near present day Monticello (western boundary), eastward to the Mancos River (eastern boundary), and down river to the San Juan River near Farmington, New Mexico.

The Blue Mountain Range covered a huge expanse of country; there were several large cattle outfits operating in this area. With a herd numbering around thirty thousand head, the largest spread was owned and operated by the Carlisle family. A herd of this size was a management headache under any circum-stances, and a spring cattle drive is one occasion where every precaution had to be taken. For one week in the spring, while the Carlisle herd was drifting through the little town of Mancos on their way to summer pasture in the Blue Mountains, the school was closed down. The half-wild longhorn mix that made up the herd was too unpredictable to be considered safe and manageable around children.

From the herds of cattle being driven through the area, Alex Calhoun was able to purchase the supply of beef he needed to keep the slaughter and delivery of his product on a dependable schedule. The demand for beef seemed always to exceed the supply. In time, Calhoun was hard-pressed to keep up with the ever increasing population of the mining towns. By 1885, the town of Telluride alone could consume more beef in one day than could be delivered in a week; the need for expansion was never more obvious. Calhoun acquired about ten acres of land not more than five miles outside of Telluride. On a place called Turkey Creek Mesa he built his first slaughterhouse. On a forty acre parcel along the San Miguel River, below the mouth of Bear Creek, another slaughterhouse was built which he called the "lower" or "winter" place. Since he was well set up now to butcher large numbers of cattle, his remaining task was to get them delivered regularly.

Billy Randall was one of the early day cowboys who drifted into the Norwood country shortly after 1880. Taking his wages mostly in cattle and trying to get a start in the cow business the same as a lot of other men, he was a working cowboy for a few years. The range was free and plentiful, and a man could just turn his cattle loose and let them range as they pleased. Drifting the cattle to the high country in the summer kept them from overgrazing the intermediate range where most of the roundups were held. In the fall, when the cattle drifted down from the high country, they were gathered by the cowboys; the calves were branded, and anything to be sold was cut back and later driven to the railroad for shipping to market. Steers were the principal product for sale, and the big cattle outfits rarely sold any animal under three years of age. When the fall roundup and shipping were over, the remaining cattle were gathered and driven to the lower elevations to spend the winter. In the spring, all the cattle owners would meet and gather off the winter range and drive the cattle to the intermediate range. Sometime in early July, yet another general roundup was held, and all the calves born since the fall ride were branded

Branding cattle near Lone Cone in 1887. (Courtesy of Francis "Bill" Stockdale.)

before the herd was taken to the summer pasture. While the big cattle outfits could be selective in what was sold, the smaller ranch owners had to sell younger animals to have money to operate on. The smaller operators often worked for the big ranches part-time to supplement their income. It was in this fashion that Billy Randall built up his small bunch of cattle.

Since the cattle range in the west end of San Miguel County was pretty well saturated with livestock, the chances of moving in and raising a large herd were very slim; the country would only support so many cattle, and that was it. In an effort to expand, however, a man with the money could buy out other outfits in the area. Billy Randall wanted to expand, and he wanted to do it faster than he could by building up a small bunch of cattle over a period of many years.

One day Billy saddled up his horse and decided to take a ride up around Telluride where the mines were booming, and the town was growing daily. After looking around a bit, he decided that here was a place where a man with a little imagination could get started at something. A German by birth and a butcher by trade, Randall knew well the business of butchering and marketing beef carcasses. Since the town of Telluride didn't have a reliable or a sufficient supply of beef, this looked like opportunity knocking at the door. He already owned a few head of cattle and knew if he could market them in this butchered manner he could realize a higher profit than the beef would bring on the live market. When Randall heard of the new slaughterhouses that Alex Calhoun had built, he felt he had found the key to his dreams.

Getting right down to business and holding several meetings with Calhoun, Billy Randall worked out an arrangement whereby he would buy both the slaughterhouses and the land they sat on and take over Calhoun's business of supplying the Telluride area with beef. Calhoun was eager to sell off his holdings in this way because it freed several pack strings he needed to service other hard-pressed areas.

Randall began his new business in Telluride by driving a few head of cattle up from nearby Norwood. The cattle were butchered and sold to the townspeople. When the supply of beef was gone, he would ride back to Norwood and gather another small bunch, trail them to Telluride, and repeat the process. The residents of the town soon came to depend on Randall for their supply of beef. By the time Billy's business began to run smoothly, he was supplying all of the beef the town and mines could use. He did this in a very competent manner for quite a few years.

The way Billy Randall kept a supply of beef on hand for butchering forms the basis of the story that follows. It is the tale of a bunch of wild cattle from Mexico later known to all as: "The Chipmunk Steers."

A branch line of the Rio Grande Southern Railroad reached the mining town of Telluride, Colorado in the year 1890. After that, living conditions were made much easier for the inhabitants of the town, and the growth of the already sprawling community took on a more rapid pace. Prior to the coming of the railroad, all supplies for the town and the booming mines had to be hauled in with horse and oxen teams pulling the huge freight wagons. Also, the versatile mule and burro pack strings were kept plenty busy delivering supplies.

Fresh beef was one of the items that was not being delivered to the town in sufficient quantities to satisfy the demand of the people. The population of the town at this time was close to 2,500, and many large mines were in operation. Operating boarding houses for the men who worked in the mines, most of the mining companies were tremendous customers for butchered beef carcasses, but no real effort was being made by anyone to increase the supply. In its dwindling supply, beef remained almost the only meat available because the market hunters had long since harvested all the wild game within twenty miles of Telluride.

New businesses were being opened to the public almost before the buildings were completed; anyone with wares to sell and a place to dispense them was immediately in business. Among the many new businesses springing up was the one that the people had long awaited—a butcher shop with fresh meat for sale every day. Beef for the miners' bellies! This first butcher shop of any major importance in the town of Telluride was opened in 1898 by an old German butcher by the name of W. M. (Billy) Randall. The store was operated by a little Irish meatcutter named Johnny McAdams, and Randall also hired another butcher by the name of "Butch" Morgan ("Butch" being short for butcher). The brother of a well-known rancher in the Nucla area, Frank Morgan, "Butch" was a big, powerful man with a lot of ambition. When he learned the shortcuts that Randall knew, plus a few innovations of his own, he could knock down a four year-old steer, skin it, dress it out, and have it in four free-swinging quarters in less than thirty minutes and do it as long as the holding pens held cattle for butchering. Morgan could split down a beef carcass with a huge, two-handed cleaver, usually in five strokes. No saws were used, and there was no mechanized equipment for hoisting and handling, just block and tackles and hand power.

When "Butch" was cutting up pork or lamb loins he used a much smaller, one-handed cleaver and worked so quickly with it, that with a *zip-zip-zip* the loin was cut into chops; he cut with such accuracy as to leave each chop almost exactly the same width. (All the butchering tools used by "Butch" Morgan, including the big, old, two-handed cleaver are in possession of young Frank Morgan of Nucla, who took over his Dad's ranch and cattle operation when his dad went into retirement.)

"Butch" Morgan worked for Billy Randall for twelve or thirteen years and helped Randall design and build a big new slaughterhouse up on Turkey Creek Mesa. This slaughterhouse replaced an earlier one built by Alex Calhoun around 1885. Morgan was able to manage the slaughterhouse very well; this left Randall free to manage the buying of cattle to keep a steady supply of stock on hand.

With every passing day, the job of keeping the butcher shop supplied with beef was growing. Billy Randall scoured the countryside for cattle to buy, and, even though there were fifty five ranches on Wilson Mesa at this time, the supply of cattle for slaughter was slowly running out. Billy was forced to buy cattle farther and farther away from Telluride.

The pressure of supplying the beef for the butcher shop brought Randall down to Norwood to buy the cattle outfit of Harry Adsit, who was running about five thousand head. On June 7, 1900, the sale was completed. Who but Randall himself would have believed that the cowboy who had driven a few small bunches of cattle out of there fifteen years before would be back with the money to buy out the biggest cattle operation in the entire area.

Now, with the big new slaughterhouse on Turkey Creek Mesa just completed, and a large supply of cattle available, Billy Randall was ready to supply all of the beef the town and mines could use. The railroad was running all the way into Telluride now. By loading his cattle at Placerville, Billy had a cheap, fast way to deliver fat cattle to his holding pastures at the mouth of Turkey Creek in the South Fork of the San Miguel River Canyon. The cattle were kept here until they were needed at the slaughterhouse up on the Mesa.

For a couple of years all went well, and the demand for beef was still on the upswing. Because the cattle that were purchased from Harry Adsit were rapidly decreasing in number, something had to be done quickly to ensure an ever present supply of fat cattle. Billy Randall decided to go to Old Mexico and buy cattle there. He knew he could buy them at ridiculously low prices and get large herds all under one brand, thus complying with border crossing regulations. Once the cattle grew fat on the lush mountain grass of San Miguel County, Randall imagined they could be slaughtered and sold at a very nice profit.

After buying somewhere between 1,000 and 1,500 head of cattle near Sonora, Mexico, Billy Randall loaded the small, snakey, wild cattle onto the railroad cars headed for the railhead at Dolores, Colorado, which was the closest railhead to the area where the cattle were to be pastured. Many of the railroad cars had faulty doors that flew open on the long rough journey to Colorado. Legend has it that these Mexican cattle literally "greased the rails" from El Paso, Texas to Dolores, Colorado. After jumping off or falling out, perhaps some cattle survived

Cowboys at dinner on roundup in 1887. Billy Randall is the cowboy in the right foreground. (Courtesy of the Colorado Historical Society.)

and roamed around the area, wherever it happened to be. Upon seeing one of these wily creatures for the first time, some perplexed cowboy probably described the animal as "a cross between a barbed wire fence and a hard winter." In spite of the rickety, old cattle cars, however, the majority of the herd made the trip in fair shape. After they were fed for a few days, they started on the long trail to the Lone Cone and North Mountain ranges of western San Miguel Country. Two of Billy Randall's cowboys, Bob Caldwell and Jode Woods, were on hand to help unload the cattle about eight miles east of Dolores where the tracks ran close alongside a steep hillside. When the doors of the stock cars were thrown open, the wild cattle jumped onto the hillside and were then herded up the hill and onto the trail to summer pasture.

These cattle were of all colors. Many were black and white, some brindle, some roan. Others were red or gray or even shades of yellow or dun. Besides being downright mean and hard to handle, one thing they all had in common was a dark stripe down their backs, hence the nickname "Chipmunk Steers." Another trait that clinched the nickname for these cattle was that after they started getting fat and frisky, about the only way they were ever seen was with their tails straight up in the air—disappearing from sight into the brush and timber, just like a chipmunk.

This bunch of "Chipmunk Steers" was not made up entirely of steers, however. There were many cows with calves, some bulls of all ages, and almost 1,000 steers and heifers. Ranging from yearlings on up to five and six year-olds, the steers were of all ages as well. As the cattle were being trailed in from Dolores, there were many weak and crippled animals that had to be dropped off along the way, as well as the cows that were having calves. It took about a week of trailing for the herd to reach the destination. A few days after arriving at the summer range, a couple of cowboys were sent back to try and round up the cattle that had been left behind. The cowboys often told of riding all the way back to Dolores without seeing hide nor hair of the "hospital bunch" as they had been labeled. The wily, Mexican animals had long since taken to the heavy brush and eventually would drift to such far off places as Bluff, Utah; some headed back to Dolores, and many roamed in the places between there and everywhere.

Subsequently turned loose on the new range, the cattle grew and waxed fat on the succulent forage. Native Bluestem and Bluegrass as high as a horse's knees sure was an improvement over the cactus and Jimson Weed the Mexican cattle had been used to.

If these Mexican cattle that arrived in Dolores in a weak and emaciated condition were difficult to gather and hold, one can imagine how spooky and wild they would become once they were fattened and healthy and had a whole new world to range around in. There wasn't a fence anywhere in the high country to stop cattle from drifting; the only thing that limited a steer's roaming was that sooner or later he would settle down and call a spot home. Even after many miles of being chased and driven around he would always return to this place of his own choosing. Escaping from cowboys and avoiding capture soon became yet another of the familiar traits of these "Chipmunk Steers."

The first summer, many of the steers were gathered and trailed to the slaughterhouse on Turkey Creek Mesa above Telluride where they would be butchered and sold. This was a difficult process because these Mexican steers were as fleet and agile as deer and quite capable of outrunning good saddle horses. They soon learned to duck the cowboys by outrunning them to the rough breaks where they could hide in the brush and rough terrain. Getting away once or twice was about all the steers needed to do to become regular outlaws. When winter came, some of the steers drifted to the lower ranges with the domestic cattle where they ranged wide and free; many of them never left the winter ranges. The rims and canyons and rough timbered benches may have reminded them of their Mexican homeland. Since the steers hid out so much of the time and always ducked at the sight of man, it seemed that their numbers were dwindling faster than was expected. This prompted the foreman of the Spectacle outfit to conclude that they were about out of cattle. This hardly seemed possible since only about one fourth of the original number had been sold, but no amount of hard riding and roping could gather more than just a few of them; this only seemed to scatter them wider.

Along about this time a young cowboy, raised in the Blue Mountains of Utah, and well educated in the ways of wild cattle, came in the area and made it known at the Spectacle Ranch that he was available to try his hand at gathering the remnants of the "Chipmunk Steers." His name was Fred Sharp, and he was immediately offered the job at top wages plus a commission on any Mavericks (unbranded cattle that are past weaning age) that he gathered. As they took up with the wild cattle, the Mavericks were starting to get rather plentiful around the country. Given his pick of the best saddle horses the Spectacle outfit owned, Fred Sharp was told to select an assistant who would also be well mounted and well paid. He chose as his partner, Dewey Greager, a young cowboy, who was fresh up from the Paradox country and who was already employed breaking horses on the Spectacle ranch. With two superbly trained Airedales, these two men delivered a steady supply of the "Chipmunk Steers," along with native cattle and a sprinkling of newly branded Mavericks to the slaughterhouse. How happy old Billy Randall must have been when he once again had the gambrels of his slaughterhouse filled with fat carcasses and a wagon load of beef quarters on its way to the markets of Telluride!

For several years, it took a tremendous amount of work on the part of these two cowboys to round up those wild Mexican cattle. The way the two cowboys worked with the Airedale dogs was to get out just after daybreak and ride through the country where cattle were grazing. There were always quite a few of the Mexican critters mingling with the native cattle. At the first

12

sight of a man on horseback, they would head for the wild, rough areas and try to hide. When this happened, Fred would set the dogs after the fleeing cattle. As soon as the dogs had reached the first animal, one would go for the head and the other for the heels. The dog at the heel would grab hold just above the hocks of a hind leg, and the other would grab hold of the steer's nose. No amount of fighting and pawing by the animal could dislodge them. (This is the work these dogs were trained for, and each knew his job well.) With unbelievable tenacity, the dogs would stay right on a steer until he quit fighting. Having never been around any dogs before, the cattle were terrified by the Aire dales. When those two dogs brought a wild steer into the

A bunch of cowboys ready to start for a Lone Cone roundup. (Courtesy of the Colorado Historical Society.)

bunch, he was plenty glad to stay there; no amount of cutting expertise could get him out of the bunch while the dogs were around. The steers would go right to the middle of the bunch and try to "mother up" to anything handy. Thinking that the herd was protection they would stay there. Some of the steers had to be roped and led, but most of them could be controlled within a bunch of domestic cattle, especially under the watchful eyes of the two dogs. In this manner that they had perfected, Dewey would drift the bunch along on a predetermined route while Fred would ride the rough country with the two dogs and run the wild cattle out to the herd. In this way, the two men could pick up a dozen or more each day and then take the entire gather to the slaughterhouse once a week.

Many of the steers that had eluded their captors long enough to attain full growth and sprout a respectable set of horns (many reaching a spread of six feet) also developed some very mean streaks. They could put on a show of viciousness and downright hatred of cowboys that could hardly be equaled by the notorious Cape Buffalo and Rhino of Africa. An episode that I recall clearly occurred when a wild old Mexican steer came within inches of killing my father's horse. Had that happened, my dad would have been at the mercy of the steer's needle-sharp horns and hoofs. The old steer had murder in his heart; it seemed that nothing but the blood of the cowboy fresh upon his horns would satisfy him.

One summer day my father and several cowboys were riding on North Mountain in the vicinity of Spencer Lake and Round Mountain. They spotted a big, wild-looking steer up on the east side of Round Mountain and stopped to watch him. All of the cowboys present agreed that he was an old outlaw that had been roaming around the upper end of Salt Arroyo and Lake Canyon for quite a few years. He had been given a wide berth by the cowboys because of his unpredictable nature, cussed meanness, and ability to outsmart the men who tried to take him in. On this particular day, it appeared that the old steer had gotten himself into a tricky situation. It looked as if a cowboy might be able to chase him out of the brush and down into the flats where the other cowboys could get their ropes on him. My father figured he could do the job of getting the steer out of the brush. So, he made his way along a trail that would bring him out on top of Round Mountain, and, most important of all, above the steer (which is where he wanted to be). This all worked out fine. As he worked his way in the thick brush, his maneuvering was clearly visible to the men down below. The old steer wasn't cooperating any at all, and his sullen attitude portended some real trouble. Suddenly, one of the men down below, a cowboy by the name of Horace Joseph, yelled up to Dad that the steer had changed course. Working his way around in the thick brush until he was above Dad, he looked as if he was preparing to charge. The odds were all with the outlaw steer now, and Dad knew full well that his only route to safety was to head his horse headlong off the mountainside and outrun the critter to the bottom. This is apparently just what the steer had in mind, too, because he fell right in behind Dad's horse. Bellowing his rage and hate, he tried to gore the horse through the flank and hindquarters. Dad's black Mustang must have suddenly realized that death was only inches away. With his tail between his legs and the bit clenched tight in his teeth, the horse came down through that brush and rocky steep ground like the "mill tails of Hades." When they reached open ground, the horse ducked off on one trail, and the steer went whistling by on another. The steer was out in the open now, and the cowboys soon had their ropes on him. Forcing him into a corral, they tied him up. When my father went up on that hillside, the plan had been to try and stay above the steer and just work him down to the bottom. Dad got him down off the hill and into the open alright, but it certainly was done with a bit more risk and fanfare than Dad had intended that day. Dad often remarked that during those brief moments, he came closer to death than at any other time in his life.

When I was just a youth, I remember reading a story by an author of western lore about a young Norwood cowboy roping a "Chipmunk Steer" on the winter range known as Wild Steer Mesa. (It is likely that the mesa got its name from the many wild steers that roamed there.) Although most of these wild cattle died back in the breaks of old age, a few old relics of these steers were still to be seen around the country as late as 1915. Hundreds of the steers that had really turned wild, however, were hunted down with rifles just for their horns. Today, a number of ranch houses still have horns from a "Chipmunk Steer" decorating a living room archway. The steers drifted so far and wide over the years that sets of horns are just as apt to be found in a barn in Blanding or Bluff, Utah as in a garage in La Sal, Utah, or even in a saloon down in Gateway, Colorado. Norwood and Telluride may even boast a set or two of the prize horns.

The "Chipmunk Steers" were excellent leaders when gentle enough to handle, and a few were used in this manner. Mr. Ed Lavender, an early day cattleman of this area and stepfather of the author, David Lavender, had an old "Chipmunk Steer" that led his herds from Paradox Valley to the Lone Cone each spring for many years. A majestic animal with beautiful, wide, sweeping horns, the steer was highly regarded by the cowboys who knew of him. Being of a restless nature with a long-legged, rangy-type body, he would outdistance the shorter legged, squatty-built Herefords. He often had to be held back so the other cattle wouldn't lose sight of him; his value as a leader would be lost if the herd couldn't keep him in sight.

After sixteen or so years in operation, Randall could rightfully call his cattle venture a success. Without him the people in the Telluride area might have had sowbelly and beans instead of their Sunday pot roast. Those steers that hid out and stayed on the winter range furnished many a meal for the early day Uranium miners of the lower mining district. Even down-at-the-heel homesteaders, who were forced by starvation to leave their sagging fences and rotting lean-to's, probably staved off their final, bitter ending by hunting down one of these wild, line-backed, multi-colored "Chipmunk Steers."

(**Author's note:** The entire stock and contents of the Telluride Butcher Shop were swept away and lost in the rampaging Coronet Creek flood of July 27, 1914. After the loss of the butcher shop, Billy Randall abandoned the slaughterhouse and sold his brand and cattle to Gord Galloway, who was a prominent Norwood rancher. Once again, the old Spectacle brand [first brought to this area in 1885 by the partnership of Adsit and Porter] was back in Norwood. Once again, it was part of the largest cattle outfit in the area.)

Chapter 2

A TWELVE DOLLAR MOUNTAIN LION

In Norwood's early days, there were several men who trapped fur-bearing animals. In the winter, trapping was their only source of income. Along with the usual coyotes, bobcats, and foxes, there were quite a few mountain lions; the hunters who really went after them could catch twenty or thirty in one winter.

John Morton wasn't a lion hunter really, but he had very good luck trapping bobcats. One day, a local resident, Mrs. James Nix, told Morton she would pay him twelve dollars for a mountain lion hide. There was one stipulation, however—no bullet holes! Mrs. Nix wanted to use the hide as a decoration for her living room and wanted it to be in perfect condition.

Morton kept this in mind while he was running his trap lines. Twelve dollars was a veritable mint for one lion pelt, and he sure could use the money.

The Naturita Canyon rim, which runs a couple of miles west of Norwood, was the most productive of the many trapping areas. A natural route of travel for predatory animals, it boasted huge rocks and slabs that fell from the rims and created an abundance of cover which was these predators' number one priority. Concealment and protective coloration are their main assets to survival. A tawny-colored lion lying on a sandstone rimrock is not easily seen. There are so many natural caves and places to hide in that the animals traveling these routes feel quite safe.

The Mule Deer (principal food supply of the mountain lion) like to lay along the Canyon rims where they can survey the country below them. It is very difficult to surprise a deer from below. If spooked from above, a deer will just jump off the rim (where they can) and disappear from sight. Also, the breezes that carry scents to the deer seem to flow down the rims. A lot of small animals den up under the rims, too, which makes the area not only a good place to trap for predators but good hunting ground for the predators themselves.

A couple of weeks after Mrs. Nix's offer, Morton was checking some traps he had under the rim. As he approached one of his bobcat sets, he could see a mountain lion which seemed to be caught in his trap. When he got closer, he could see that the lion was caught by two toes and wasn't fighting the trap. Here was twelve dollars staring him right in the face; Morton's mind raced as he tried to figure out how to kill the animal without putting a hole in the hide.

John was carrying a short-barreled .22 single shot that he used to dispatch trapped animals, but he didn't dare use it on the lion. Instead, he trimmed up a good, strong, pinion (strong, native wood) club and started moving in on the lion. He had plenty of trouble keeping his dog from charging into the lion. The dog was a small, short-haired terrier that was mighty long on nerve. As Morton and his dog advanced toward the lion, the animal kept backing away until he reached the end of the trap chain. Then, without hesitation he sprang on top of John and knocked him to the ground. The lion began mauling and chewing him up. Luckily, Morton's heavy winter clothing was keeping the lion's teeth and claws from penetrating the flesh and bone underneath.

Forgetting the club, Morton desperately tried to get away from the lion. The little dog decided to get into the act again and jumped into the lion's face. The terrier was slapped about twenty feet down the hill, but that dog came right back to the attack. In this brief time, Morton scrambled to safety, but he had to make a quick grab for his rifle as the dog and the lion were again going at it tooth and nail.

The dog was sent spinning through the air again; for a brief second the lion stood still. Knowing he had to shoot the lion to save the dog's life, Morton snapped a quick shot at the lion's head, and the animal dropped to the ground, dead. Morton turned the body over to examine the dead animal. Relieved to be out of his predicament, he was still curious whether there was a chance he might still hope for that twelve dollar reward on the hide. As luck would have it, the bullet had entered the brain through an eyeball. In an unlikely turn of events, Morton had gotten Mrs. Nix a mountain lion pelt—one that was without a bullet hole in it and worth twelve dollars.

Chapter 3

THREE AGAINST THE STORM

"My heart's in the highlands, my heart is not here,
my heart's in the highlands, chasing the deer. . . ."

The Lone Cone Mountain. Mystical as it is beautiful. Breeder of great storms. Father of many tragedies. Through the years there have been countless stories of climbers who, after reaching the top of the rugged peak, were struck dead by a lightning bolt. Men in rescue parties have been killed in the very same way as the victim they tried to rescue; sheepherders have frozen to death in their bedrolls during heavy snowstorms when temperatures hit bottom within a few hours. Many cowboys, too, had their close calls when a fast moving storm would catch them miles away from camp. Only the instincts of their saddle horses brought them safely to their line shacks and the lifesaving warmth of fire. Many more near-miss tragedies have been credited to the moods of this great mountain, including the tale that is related here about three young elk hunters. Two of the hunters were my brothers, Floyd and Oran Greager. The other man was a young house builder by the name of Bill Cline, who, with his wife Claireen, had just moved to the area. It happened that Claireen and Oran's wife, Jan, were long-time friends.

It was difficult for the working men to get together at the same time for a day of elk hunting, but they finally agreed to do it on the last day of elk season. It could have very easily been the last day of their lives.

Ranging in age between twenty-six and thirty-six, these men were already old hands at hunting and camping out. Raised in the mountains, they had grown up climbing the peaks for thrills and hunting the high meadows and spruce for deer and elk. They were quite capable of dealing with adverse weather conditions and had done so many times in the past. Now, adverse weather is one thing, but the storm of a lifetime brings on the kind of conditions that can cause a fellow to question his survival skills. Prior to this day, the weather had been clear and not really too cold. During the early part of elk season, a small storm had brought about four inches of snow which, at least in the open areas, had mostly melted. On this particular day (this last day of elk season of 1955), mother nature decided to throw away her rule book and unleash one of the worst snowstorms to hit the area in more years than could be remembered. In just eight hours, over two feet of snow would fall; when the storm abated, the temperature would drop sixty degrees in four hours.

The three hunters had decided to hunt the northwest area of the Lone Cone at an elevation of between 10,000 and 11,000 feet. Floyd and his wife, Marie, had driven up there the previous Sunday to scout the area, and the hunting conditions looked good to them. Since a logging crew had been working in this region for two seasons, they had built many roads back into the highest part of the heavily timbered north slope of the mountain. Many hunters used these roads to get back into the better hunting areas. These three were no exception and would use one of the highest roads to approach the mountain peak.

As the star-studded sky presaged a clear day, the three men left Norwood before daylight. With so little snow on the ground and not anticipating any bad weather, the hunters were outfitted minimally, medium-weight jackets and cotton shirts, blue jeans, light underwear, and leather hiking boots (adequate clothing for normal hunting weather but clearly inadequate for what they ultimately would encounter). Using his pickup, Oran was hauling a pack horse into the area in case they needed help retrieving an elk or two . . . or three. In Oran's pickup, the hunters started up the logging road.

With the hunt underway and the men several miles from the pickup, a storm blew in. When the weather started looking bad, they discussed moving to lower country or at least out of the heavy, black, spruce belt they would have to go through to reach the truck. Because it was the last day of elk hunting season and the three friends had looked forward to spending time together, they didn't want to give up hunting quite so soon. Perhaps the storm threat was just a brief squall and would blow over. Better judgment didn't prevail; the men continued to hunt. At about four P.M., it was snowing so hard that nearly a foot of snow had already piled up in the timber; visibility was down to a few yards. Even though the men hadn't wanted to give up hunting quite so soon, they decided that they didn't they want to die quite so soon either, and they finally started back to try to find Oran's pickup. Already wet to the knees, they still had to force their way past heavily laden spruce boughs for two and a half miles. Wet to the waist now, they realized it was nearing six P.M. and already dark; the temperature was starting to fall very fast.

Now, a native to this area uses the instinct of dead reckoning to decide how to get from one place to another. After all, a guy doesn't need a compass to get around in his own backyard. Luckily, this instinct was alive and well in the two brothers, and it guided them all to a logging road. They came out of the timber about a quarter mile above Oran's pickup. As they walked down the road, an old abandoned log cutter's shack came into view a short distance from the road. Strictly a summer habitation, it was very flimsy in structure—without panes or a door. Its roof was fairly sagging under two feet of wet, heavy snow. The three hunters joked a little about what it would be like to have to stay in such a place.

When they reached the pickup, Oran opened the rack, jumped the mare in, and closed it. Wet, cold and shivering too much to talk, they all got in the pickup cab. Oran put the key in the switch and turned it to *on*. The engine started cranking, but there was no sign of life. After pumping the gas pedal a little and pulling out the choke some more, he cranked the engine again for about a minute. Still, not a cylinder had fired; the men were all a little perplexed. A truck that had proved to be the most dependable vehicle around was now unable to fire even once. The gas gauge showed that there was plenty of fuel; the battery was strong and cranked the engine at a good clip. After another minute of cranking to no avail, the men discussed the situation and agreed that either the gas line was frozen or there was ice in the carburetor. One thing they knew all too well was that they couldn't sit there for very much longer. In the back, the mare was also soaking wet everywhere but under the saddle and was getting restless and stamping around a lot to shake away the cold.

After getting out of the vehicle, Floyd somehow managed to get the top off the carburetor with a screwdriver and wire pliers. Sure enough, the float chamber had a lot of ice in it, and the needle valve was frozen shut. That meant not one drop of gas could get to the engine. With fingers so cold and numb that they were beyond feeling, Floyd extracted the needle valve and held a match to it to warm it. He was sure that the heated needle valve, once returned to its seat in the float chamber, would thaw the ice blocking the tiny hole and permit the flow of gas to the carburetor. This seemed like a great plan. Unfortunately, when your fingers are like ten sticks of wood, the odds of dropping what you're holding run high. That is exactly what happened next. The three men spent the next half hour trying to find the needle valve in the proverbial haystack. Not equipped with a flashlight and with two feet of new snow, a pitch black night, and the snow still falling hard, the men realized there didn't seem to be much use in looking anymore. The men were frightfully cold, and the temperature was steadily, rapidly dropping. Before midnight, it would reach twenty-eight degrees below zero.

By now it was about 8 P.M., and the hunters had to come up with an idea and quick. They hadn't had anything to eat since noon when they had stopped hunting long enough to eat a sandwich and an apple and discuss the weather. Their disappointment over the loss of their transportation was a hard blow to cope with. Nearly as important to them as their own welfare was that of their horse. A valuable quarterbred mare, she had a bright future ahead of her.

By this time there were only two choices left. They could trudge through the deep snow down the main road out of the area and try to make it six miles to the O.A. Greager summer cabin. Their other choice was to backtrack to the old log cutter's shack, build a big fire, and try to see the night through. The thought that someone might come looking for them had not yet entered their heads. Their thoughts were mainly on their own survival.

I had hunted with these three men on many occasions. The only reason I wasn't with them on this trip was because I was saving my elk tag for the later post-season in the Dallas Divide Area. As a group of hunters, we had a method for hunting that northwest part of the Lone Cone. We would go up to the highest road accessible by pickup, and all but one would be dropped off to spread out and hunt in a wide sweep down the north slope. The lone man would take the vehicle to a lower point where eventually everyone would meet up again. The idea was always to try to come out of the brush on the old Circle Cross Ranch about five miles below. In that way, we could hunt the spruce belt, then a couple of miles of aspen, and eventually the scrub oak brush for a couple more miles. If the game aren't in the spruce, chances are they will be found lower. It's best to always start in the spruce when you're fresh and strong because this area is the roughest. No roads exist in there, no trails can be followed after it snows. The fallen timber is very thick on the ground and is three or four layers deep in some places. With a good covering of snow it is certainly no place to be after dark, because the chances of slipping down into a windfall and breaking a leg are very real. Under normal circumstances, our group had often made this trip down off the north face of the Lone Cone in about an hour and a half. It's actually a pretty quick way to get from timberline down to the main highway from Norwood to Dolores. Normal circumstances meant traveling during the daylight hours and not through two or three feet of snow in the bitter cold.

While to Floyd, the two choices clearly seemed the only ones, Oran and Bill thought the best idea was to walk that familiar route down the north slope of the old mountain. Floyd pointed out that the conditions around them presently were a wee bit more adverse, to say the least, than they had been on the many occasions that the young men had successfully weaved their way down through the thick forest. Even if they could somehow make it, which Floyd doubted, they would still end up at the Circle Cross in a deserted cabin which they would have to break into in order to build a fire. A more sensible idea would be to try to walk five or six miles down the road to Uncle Oswald's summer cabin and break into that place to build a fire, but Floyd didn't favor this idea either. They still had a valuable mare to deal with, and they sure as heck couldn't take her down through the timber. The old log cutter's shack was really the only reasonable alternative; therefore, they unanimously decided to return to the flimsy hut that had been the brunt of their jokes several hours earlier. The mare was unloaded from the pickup, and they all trudged their way back to the shack.

Once there, they ripped boards up off the floor; with the dry sticks they found underneath, the men got a fire started. After more boards were broken up and added to the fire, the mare was led into the back of the cabin so she could start drying out as well.

When a blocked chimney quickly caused the little room to fill with smoke, it became impossible to remain. The horse was coughing, and everyone's eyes were burning and watering. Bill and Floyd hoisted Oran up onto the roof where he tore out two boards near the chimney stack; presently the smoke cleared some, and they were all able to go back inside and keep the fire going. They were resigned to stay here all night. Hungry, tired, and cold, they had to remain in a smoke-filled, little ramshackle of a cabin with a prized mare who was surely feeling no better than the men. For all their efforts, the fire was hardly big enough to ward off the chill of the bitter cold night. In the quiet, dark coldness, the three men's thoughts turned to their worried wives and children. At this time Floyd and Oran were also partners in a business, the Lone Cone Bar and Cafe.

By about eight P.M. my phone was ringing pretty regularly with calls from nervous wives who knew better than to feel comfortable about their husbands being gone so long. For the men to be late from a hunting trip was not unusual; to be late in weather like this surely meant something had gone wrong. Floyd's wife Marie arrived at my house at about 10:30 P.M. She wanted to know if there was anything I could do. I asked her if she wanted to go look for them and if she knew the exact area where they were planning to hunt. Marie was pretty sure she knew the location of the logging road which turned off from the main haulage road out of the area. Certain she could recognize it, she wanted to start searching.

Because I had to find a four-wheel drive vehicle, I immediately thought of Hoyt Brown, who had a new Jeep station wagon. Since I was working as a log cutter for him at the time,

I felt he would let me use it, especially under these circumstances. I called Hoyt at 11:00 P.M. Although I woke him from a sound sleep, he readily agreed when I explained the serious nature of my request. Marie picked up a couple of quart thermos bottles of coffee and a sack of sandwiches from the cafe. Dressed in practically all of the warm clothing we owned, carrying extra blankets and coats, and with the blessings of the other wives, we headed on our way.

We had to travel thirty-three miles to where the pickup was stalled. When Marie saw it, she started getting scared. She knew the elk hunters were in serious trouble. Fortunately, the snow had stopped falling at about the time the three men and the horse had left the pickup and headed for the old shack. Marie and I were able to see their tracks in the light from our vehicle's headlights. It was past midnight now, and the thermometer on the windshield of the Jeep read twenty-eight degrees below zero. The men in the cabin had just about given up being found before daylight. When we drove up, they were ready to set fire to the whole cabin in an effort to keep warm. To say that the men were glad to see us would be a serious understatement; relieved doesn't describe their emotions either. The men were saved from a potential tragedy, and they knew it. Coffee and sandwiches disappeared in a flash. With extra coats on now and wrapped in blankets, the three men were helped into the warm Jeep. This was the first time any of them had sat down in almost eighteen hours.

Just then, I heard a loud explosion like a rifle shot from back in the timber. We all thought someone else was in the area and might be signaling for help. This old mountain could boast of many lost hunters over the years. Taking a flashlight out of the Jeep, I walked back into the trees to where the sound had come. Although I kept walking and yelling every little while, not another sound was heard. Suddenly, I noticed a large spruce tree had split open in the sap ring. The temperature in the forest dropped so fast and so low that the sap ring of the big tree had burst open with a loud explosion. Winter claimed the forest in unusual ways.

I made my way back to the Jeep, and we prepared to get the pickup back to town. The mare was dry now since the three men had taken turns rubbing her down with the saddle blankets and drying them by the fire. After loading the mare into the pickup, we hooked the Jeep onto the front end and started out. Since I was the driest and dressed the warmest, I rode in the pickup to steer it on the way to town. Because I couldn't run the engine, we couldn't use the heater or defroster. Soon, there were no headlights once the weakened battery gave out. All I had for company was a frost scraper. The trip back to Norwood took over two hours to make and was an extremely cold ride. Because there was no protection for the horse, we couldn't drive very fast. With the temperature down to nearly thirty degrees below zero and with the wind that our caravan would certainly create, the potential chill factor could very easily frost the horse's lungs. We knew that we would have to keep our speed well under fifteen miles an hour.

By the time we arrived at the place where the mare was being kept, I know I was nearly as cold as she. I led her around the barnyard in a good trot until we were both warmed up a bit. The mare readily went into her stall where she practically inhaled a bucket of rolled oats. I stood there for a few minutes watching her. More than once, she looked up at me with a knowing expression as if to tell me that she understood the peril of our earlier circumstances. She was clearly grateful to be back in her safe, warm stall. While I was caring for the mare, the rest of the party went into the house and called their wives to let them know they were safely back in town and would be home soon.

It was four A.M. before anyone of us got to bed that morning—exactly twenty-four hours since the three hunters had left their beds to set out on a routine elk hunt. Miraculously, none of the men suffered any frostbite nor did any of them contract pneumonia or even become sick with a cold.

All's well that ends well, so the expression goes. But in the re-telling of my brothers' ominous adventure I must tell of how often I have wondered about a certain moment—a moment in which the hunters, each exhausted and thankful in the safety and warmth of his own comfortable bed, started drifting off to sleep, recalling their adventure, and finally realizing that not one of them had seen an elk during this entire ordeal.

Chapter 4

THE SPECTACLE BRAND

A Colorful History

Brand registration by the State of Colorado began on April 15, 1885. Registration by counties had been in effect for several years before that time, and brands were then published in the first Colorado Brand Book. The length of time that a brand had been used prior to this time would be hard to trace unless a person had some direct family ties going way back. In all the years of research, I have never been able to find an old county Brand Book.

The first person to record ownership of the Spectacle brand was Harry B. Adsit. The year he started using it is not known but research indicates that it was most likely around 1875. It is known from his personal records and files that Harry Adsit spent the winter of 1876 in Del Norte, Colorado, on his way from the San Luis Valley to the gold country around Silverton and Rico. Very shortly after this, Mr. Adsit went into the cattle business with a partner, Mr. Porter. They registered the Spectacle brand in San Juan County on April 15, 1885.

About that same year or possibly the summer of 1886, they moved their operation to the Norwood area and established their headquarters' camp on the west side of the Lone Cone. The stream that ran by the camp came to be known as Spectacle

Creek. The other places that were named for the Spectacle outfit are located on what was used as the winter range: Adsit Draw, Spectacle Draw, Spectacle Reservoir, and Chipmunk Reservoir. These are all located in the lower end of Dry Creek Basin at the base of Monogram Mesa.

At this time, Harry Adsit was running about five thousand head of cattle; this was the largest operation in the entire area. He was also a great lover of horses and raised many fine thoroughbreds. If Adsit took a liking to someone, it is said that he almost always made them a gift of a nice, young horse.

Along in the early summer of 1888, which was one of Adsit's peak years in the cattle business, a couple of young cowboys rode into the ranch and asked about work. One of them, a very nice-appearing lad, gave his name as Robert Leroy Parker of Circle Valley, Utah. The other, an equally good-looking young man, introduced himself as Matt Warner of Beaver, Utah. Adsit gave the two young men jobs punchin' cows, and they ended up staying on for about a year. "Bud" Parker, as he was called by the other cowboys, came to be well-liked and respected as a good cowhand, but he had one big fault; he was always looking around for faster money than the thirty dollars a month he earned punchin' cows.

In the fall of 1888, while working for Adsit, Parker slipped away and built a well-concealed corral on Stockdale Point. One day he corralled about thirty head of steers that belonged to Alfred Dunham. What Parker intended to do with the steers one can only guess. A pretty alert cattleman, Dunham discovered the missing steers the next day and turned them back to pasture. Somehow he found out who built the corral and penned up his steers. Although he seriously considered getting the sheriff and having Parker arrested for larceny of livestock, he changed his mind after giving it some thought. He had gotten his steers back with no harm done, so he dropped the idea. As it turned out, Alfred Dunham lived to be quite an old man. Had he gotten the sheriff after "Bud" Parker (who was later known as the infamous outlaw, "Butch" Cassidy), he might not have lived to see his thirty-fifth birthday.

One day early the next summer, "Bud" Parker asked Mr. Adsit if he could draw his wages because he was thinking of moving on. Having taken quite a liking to the young cowboy, Adsit wanted him to stay on. When Parker made it plain that he was leaving, Adsit gave him his pick of the young thoroughbreds. The young man selected a dapple brown, a four year-old that he had ridden since starting to work on the Spectacle Ranch. Parker had spent many hours training the horse to stand so he could be mounted from behind with a running leap to the saddle. What Harry Adsit had no way of knowing at the time was that Parker had been making plans to rob the Bank of Telluride while he was working for him the previous summer.

Later that day, "Bud" Parker rode away from the Spectacle Ranch on the dapple brown colt marked with a Spectacle brand on his left hind leg. If the colt was four in the spring of 1889, he would have been foaled in the spring of 1885; that was the year that Adsit and Porter registered the Spectacle brand and then later moved to San Miguel County. No cattleman and horsebreeder of Adsit's caliber would ever let an animal go unbranded, especially if the animal was being moved a long distance overland.

Robert Leroy Parker rode the brown colt in and out of Telluride when he robbed the Bank of Telluride on June 24th, 1889 with Matt Warner and Tom McCarty. Harry Adsit was in Telluride that very day and identified both Parker and his horse. The bank robbers had left a string of relay horses staked out over by Rico. When they got there with their loot, they turned their tired horses loose, mounted the fresh horses, and continued on their way. The sheriff of Telluride rounded up a posse and chased the bank robbers until he came upon their abandoned horses. Realizing that they could never catch the outlaws, who were now on fresh mounts, he gathered up their horses and returned with them to Telluride.

The sheriff continued to ride "Bud" Parker's horse around Telluride after that. It must have given him a sense of much needed credibility or something since the outlaws themselves had gotten completely away. When Harry Adsit found out that the sheriff had kept Parker's thoroughbred horse from the Spectacle ranch, Adsit tried very hard to get him back. However, the sheriff claimed he was the confiscated property of a fugitive and refused to give him up.

When word reached Parker that the sheriff of Telluride was riding his horse, he sent the sheriff a letter reminding him that the dapple brown colt had carried him 110 miles in twenty-four hours and had paid a dividend of $20,750 (the amount taken in the Telluride Bank robbery). Parker told the sheriff in his letter that he would be much obliged if the sheriff would deliver the horse to him at Moab, Utah. Predictably, the sheriff declined the offer and rode the horse around Telluride for many more years.

Following the robbery, Parker had wanted to go to his home in Circleville, Utah and spend some time with his family but knew that his association with the robbery would bring too much shame to them. He also knew that the law would soon be after him. For about two months, he spent his time roaming around Eastern Utah and staying out of sight, alone with his thoughts. Although they had gone their separate ways after they divided up the money, the robbers kept a line of communication open by many secretive means.

After considering the fact that all of the men involved in the Telluride Bank Robbery had been identified, Parker knew that he could no longer go by his given name. At one time, he had worked on a horse ranch in Wyoming for a man he liked quite well; that man's name was Mike Cassidy. Knowing that he had to come up with a new name, he decided that Cassidy was as good a name as any. Since Parker had worked in several

38

butcher shops and other places doing butchering jobs, he felt he was entitled to the nickname "Butch," short for butcher. With that addition, his new name became "Butch Cassidy." From that moment on and for probably the next twenty years, he was known by no other name.

Harry Adsit sold out to his partner, Porter, not long after the summer of the infamous bank robbery. Mr. Porter later gathered all of the Spectacle cattle, sold them, and moved out of the area. Although Adsit started up another cattle outfit in the Norwood area some time later, he didn't have the Spectacle brand anymore. Because Porter was still keeping up the assessments, that brand wasn't available. So, the new brands that Harry Adsit registered in 1892, were the Drag E ⚞, the Turkey Track ⚟, and the Pitchfork ⌶.

The Spectacle brand was dropped by Porter sometime before 1900, which was about the same time as Harry Adsit was selling out again. A butcher and cattleman by the name of Billy Randall bought out Adsit and found the Spectacle brand to be available. Randall registered the brand on June 13, 1900.

During the years that Billy Randall had the Spectacle brand, it came to be very well-known all over the soutwestern part of Colorado and eastern Utah—primarily because of the Mexican steers that Randall had brought north, branded with the Spectacle brand, and then turned loose in western San Miguel county. The steers became so wild that some of them were later gathered a hundred miles from where they had originally been turned loose. Most of the cowboys in the region called them the "Chipmunk Steers," but they were equally well-known as the "Spectacle Steers."

Running the Spectacle brand until 1914, Billy Randall sold out to Gord Galloway following the disastrous Cornett Creek flood in Telluride. Galloway did not keep the brand that came with the cattle outfit, however. His own Heart brand was well-known and suited him just fine.

Records indicate that the Spectacle brand was not recorded to anyone else until my father, "Dewey" Greager, registered it on May 15, 1928 after buying a hundred head of white-faced cows. These cattle were the last in the area to be marked with the Spectacles. My father still owned the brand when he died in 1947. On June 20, 1950, I transferred the brand to my name. I still own the brand along with the branding irons that were made by my dad in the summer of 1928.

Chapter 5

A COWBOY IN THE FAMILY

Most of the people who came West in the years after the Civil War did so for reasons such as avoiding religious persecution, finding business opportunities, or just following family members who had preceded them. My father came West simply because he would have died at a very early age if he had continued to live at his family's home on the East Coast. His fight with asthma and related bronchial problems lasted the full sixty-seven years of his life. Welcoming the clean, pure air of western Colorado, he adopted an invigorating, outdoor lifestyle which gave him the chance for fairly normal health that he otherwise would never have known. His parents' decision to send him to a high, dry, semi-arid climate, resulted in a bonus of fifty-five wonderful years of hard work and play and raising a very large family—years of seeing the country change from unfenced cattle range to prosperous farms and ranches and towns.

My father was one of the early cowboys of southwestern Colorado. His life story is included in this book for no simpler reason than that. While I did not necessarily learn from him what I portray and characterize in these writings, my father either knew the people personally or was actually a part of many of the situations and circumstances described within the pages of this book.

My father, Rudolph Paul Greager, was born in Manchester, New Hampshire on October 26, 1880. He was the fourth child and third son of Herman and Earnestine A. Greager; their children were born in this order: Tillie (the only girl), Herman, Oswald, Rudolph, and Albert.

At an early age Dad was afflicted with asthma which left him thin and in poor health. The damp weather of the East coast aggravated his condition, and the family doctor finally decided that Dad's life would be very short if he stayed in this type of climate. The doctor recommended sending him to Arizona or to the western slope of Colorado.

As it happened, my father's father was a member of the Mason Lodge. During the Civil War, he had made the acquaintance of another Mason from Montrose, Colorado known as Preacher Hampton. After getting in touch with him, Grandad Greager asked if he could send his son to stay with the Hampton family. Preacher Hampton said he would be happy to take Dad into his home; he would see to it that Dad received his education through the eighth grade. The Mason Lodge handled all of the transportation, and Tillie, Dad's older sister, accompanied him on the long train ride to Montrose. The year was 1893, and my father was about thirteen years old, a pretty tender age to be leaving home for a new life, way out West.

The next year went by quickly and without problems as Preacher Hampton's daughter, Emma Florence, took a tremendous liking to Dad and soon began to oversee his care. Through her efforts and direction, my father completed the eighth grade at the nearby Oak Grove School.

Around the time that Dad was finishing up in school, Emma Hampton was planning to marry Bert Albin, a big cattleman up on the Dew Drop range of the Uncompaghre. Because Emma felt that Dad was still a bit too young and inexperienced to go his own way, and since she cared for him so much, she persuaded her husband to give Dad a job on the ranch. This way, she could continue her motherly care of the boy she had grown so fond of.

Dad worked on Bert and Emma's ranch for several years and grew to be a good hand with all kinds of livestock. Bert particularly liked Dad's way with horses, and kept him well supplied with broncs to break. Many of the colts that Dad broke were sold to The United States Cavalry. During the time that Dad was working for Bert Albin, he gained sufficient reputation to be included along with some of the real cowboys of that era: Mid Hampton (who was almost Dad's foster brother), Burt Fraser, and Harry Watt. Joe Gray and Arthur Richardson were also a couple of cowboys that would ride anything that wore hair. Later on, Joe Gray became known as the only local cowboy who ever took "the buck out of a zebra."

During the Spanish-American War, on a day when Dad was breaking out yet another string of horses, a newspaper which contained an article that caught Bert's interest arrived at the ranch. The article told how Admiral Dewey had taken his flagship, *Oregon*, into Manila Bay and almost single-handedly annihilated the Spanish Fleet. The ships that managed to get away were chased far out to sea where they could no longer aid the Spanish troops in the Philippines. When Bert Albin read this he is said to have remarked, "That's about the way that Rudy has been mopping up on these broncs around here." After this everyone on the ranch began calling Dad "Admiral Dewey." The "Admiral" part was dropped before too long, and anyone who knew my father after 1898 knew him as "Dewey" Greager and were never aware that he had had any other name.

Between 1898 and 1900, my dad and another young cowboy, Jimmy Smith, worked at catching wild horses and breaking them for sale to the Cavalry. During these years, Dad became acquainted with the Billy Creek Range, which included Chaffee Draw and the head of Cow Creek. My father remarked to me many times that this was probably the roughest country that

45

God ever laid out for a cowboy to ride over.

At the turn of the century, Dad found himself working for a man by the name of Dick Nethery on Sanborn Park. Nethery was the man who taught Dad to shear sheep; this trade would prove very helpful to Dad during the later years of his life. Nethery's mark on this area of southwestern Colorado came about in a sad way. He owned a herd of goats that were one day stampeded over a high cliff in a canyon by a bunch of Norwood cattlemen. This area became known as Goat Creek.

Following his work with Nethery, Dad went to work for Gord Galloway at Bedrock and worked there until 1902. The Galloway outfit summered their cattle on the Lone Cone and Beaver Park areas and wintered them in Paradox and the surrounding country. This employment allowed my dad to become acquainted with the Young family and particularly Bertha Young, whom he later married in 1908. There was a host of people in this area with whom Dad became friends. (Many of them have stories of their own which are recounted in other chapters of this book.) They were: Bill Huff and his brother, Asa, Mel Turner, Steve Swain, Indian Henry, the Talbert family, and also the Hartmans, Clark Warden, Cy Orr, Frank White, Bob Caldwell, John Scott, Edward Pitts, Charley Wilkerson, and Chester Blackburn.

In 1902, Dad went to work for Billy Randall who operated a big slaughterhouse on Turkey Creek Mesa. To supply the slaughterhouse with beef, Randall had bought out Harry Adsit, who operated quite a large cattle outfit. To further the supply of beef, Randall also had bought a herd of Mexican cattle and brought them into the Lone Cone North Mountain country. Randall had previously recorded the Spectacle brand, and this mark was put on all of the semi-wild Mexican cattle.

The Norwood headquarters for the Spectacle outfit was about a half-mile east of town. On this ranch, a cowboy by the name of Fred Sharp first met Dad. Randall's Mexican cows had really gone wild and were spread out all over the countryside. Knowing of Sharp's skill as a cowboy, he had hired him to round up the remnants of the "The Chipmunk Steers," as they had come to be known. After watching Dad bare heel some colts around the corral, Sharp decided to take Dad in as his partner. (See Chapter one, "The Chipmunk Steers.")

After four wild years of catching these elusive cattle passed, Dad started up a business in Norwood. It was a combination Barber Shop, Saloon, and Pool Hall. He was still in the Saloon business when he married Bertha Young in 1908. Their first child and only daughter was born in Norwood on December 26, 1908. They named her La Verna Alice, which was later changed to La Verna Bertha. The house they lived in is still standing and has become the living quarters for the people who preach for and maintain the Pentecostal Church. In 1909, to supplement his income, Dad took the job of town marshal for awhile. His sons, Jack and Paul, were born during the next few years in the same house as their sister. Herman Ernest (Jack) was born July 11, 1911; Paul Rudolph was born June 22, 1912. After the voter option of 1912 which threatened to remove all saloons from the city limits, Dad moved everything to Placerville and went into partnership with Frank Graves who was an experienced saloonkeeper. Dick McKeever also had a saloon in Norwood at this time. He moved his business two miles east of town, and it became known as the "Hog Ranch," a drink-and-dance honkytonk sort of affair with about three available girls for those who wished their company. Today you will find the property occupied by the state highway garage.

Shortly after Dad moved to Placerville, he witnessed the murder of a man known as Mattiotti. He was murdered by a deputy marshal named Dan Walters. When Walters saw Dad on the back porch of the saloon, he shot twice at him. Witnesses to murder weren't supposed to be left alive. Walters did leave his witness alive, however, and escaped from the area. He was never seen around Placerville again.

With a 1912 model "T" Ford, my father operated the first taxi business in San Miguel County. Since cowboys on a party couldn't stick around for the morning train into Telluride, Dad would transport them for a price in his model "T" taxi. Much of the time his services were secured early in the evening, and he had to wait around until his fare was ready to leave. His time-waiting was often spent partying with the crowd. The taxi also hauled quite a few miners from Telluride to the coke ovens in Dry Creek Canyon or the uranium workings on Monogram Mesa.

A fourth child, Glen Ivel, was born at Placerville in the Frank Graves house on November 25, 1913. His mother never recovered from complications of childbirth, however, and she died on August 15, 1914.

Following this tragedy, Dad started selling Dodge cars for Hartman Brothers of Montrose and also obtained rights to sell Fords through the agency of Dan Pavancho of Moab, Utah. In the business of selling and demonstrating cars, Dad traveled over most of southwestern Colorado. Making many connections in Disappointment Valley, he sold a few cars there. In the process of selling a 1915 Dodge touring car to a Henry Knight, Dad was asked to demonstrate it by driving it up the old wagon road that starts at the head of Disappointment Valley and heads northeast toward Norwood. Not much more than a trail, this old road was very steep and narrow with several small, sharp switchbacks as it went right up the bottom of a draw. No one, except Dad, believed a car could make it out of there. After examining the road thoroughly, he asked Henry Knight if he would buy the car if it managed to make the hill all right. When Knight agreed, Dad went on to wager a hundred dollars that he could make the hill. This bet was promptly covered by a couple of cowboys by the names of Monte Fitch and John Hart, who were working at the time for the Crutch Outfit owned by John

Clay and Company of Kansas City, Missouri. After putting the mud chains on the car, Dad started up the old wagon road. Although he had to keep backing up to negotiate the sharp turns, and his tires spun out quite a bit over the rocky, bumpy terrain, he eventually made it over the top. Dad collected on his bet, and Mr. Knight took delivery of his new car. Failing to take the time to learn much about driving, Knight usually drove his car in only two gears: second and reverse. Since these gears were straight back and forth of each other, he saw no need to get fancy with them. Still, he could drive anywhere there was a road and in any kind of weather. Today, most of the roads he traveled back then with his touring car are considered passable only by four wheel drive vehicles or horses. In the fall of 1941, I went down the old wagon road on horseback with my good friend, the late Vernon Bankston. The road was mostly eroded away by then, but enough of it remained to prove that there had been a road there once.

The first meeting between my mother and my father was in the town of Nucla, Colorado, and it came about in this way. Mother's sister, Mamie, and her husband Baley Hurd (see Chapter ten) were living there; Baley was punching cows for Ern Maupin. Though Mother lived in Delta at the time, she had been in Placerville visiting her cousin, Hattie Beach, for a few days and decided to take the stage to Nucla and visit Mamie for awhile as well. After staying there for a few days, she took the stage on down to Ford Camp (Uravan) and visited another sister, Bertha, who was living there with her husband, Jim Williams. Jim had a pack string of Burros and was hauling salt from Bedrock to the new uranium mill in Uravan. Mother had only been with Bertha a few days when Baley sent George Stoner down with a horse to get Mother and bring her back up to Nucla. Because Mamie was about to give birth (to a boy they would name Emmett), she wanted Mother there to help around the house. Soon after the baby was born, Baley had to leave for a few days. When he returned a few days later, he was accompanied by the rowdiest bunch of cowboys you could fit into a model "T" Ford: "Dewey" Greager, Harry Watt, Walter Cade, and the stage driver, Art Richardson. They all got off at Baley and Mamie's house where they were introduced to each other. That's how Essie met "Dewey."

A short time later Mother went back to Placerville and stayed with her Aunt Ida and cousin Hattie for awhile. During this stay, Mother received a letter from her mother. It reported Floyd's (Mother's brother) approaching marriage and mentioned that she wished Mother could make it to the wedding. Somehow Dad heard of the impending need for transportation and offered to drive Mother and Hattie to Delta to the wedding. Here, Dad met Mother's parents and family on July 16, 1916. For the next few months Mom and Dad saw quite a bit of one another; on September 19, 1916, Essie Beach and Dewey Greager were married. Since they had been witnesses for Essie's brother, Floyd, and his bride Dora, Floyd and Dora returned the honor when they stood up as witnesses for Essie and Dewey.

Having sold his interest in the saloon to Frank Graves, he bought the pre-emption rights to Tom Cassity's homestead on Beaver Mesa. Dad kept his house in Placerville as well as several others over the years. Only two of the five children in Dad's second family were born in the same house. The order of the birth of the children is as follows:

Afton Arlene	11/11/17	Frank Graves house—Placerville
Floyd Beach	3/3/20	Dobler place—Placerville
Keith Armand	5/10/22	House near stockyards—Placerville
Howard Edgar	5/31/24	House near stockyards—Placerville
Oran Leonard	2/18/27	Telluride Hospital—Telluride

The first year that Dad went to work on his ranch was 1918

The Greager family ranch home on Beaver Mesa in 1926. The author spent the first six summers of his life here.

when he and Harry Watt jointly owned a bunch of cattle. When Watt sold his ranch a year later, the partnership broke up. Although Dad kept a few cattle, he made his living primarily leasing sheep from Mrs. Eva Fitzpatrick of Montrose. With summer grazing permits covering from the head of Elk Creek all the way around to the east of Woods Lake to Navajo Lake, Dad was well organized to run sheep. Out in the open, this area was above timberline and made an excellent summer range. In the spring, Dad would take a band of ewes and lamb them out at his ranch on Beaver Mesa before he summered them on this high pasture. In the fall, after the lambs were shipped, Dad would turn the band back to Mrs. Fitzpatrick, who would winter them around Montrose.

In 1928, Dad leased 2,000 head of sheep from a man by the

name of Ern Andress. Ern was sort of a partner of Ed Lavender in the sense that he farmed the Galloway ranch in Bedrock (which was owned by Lavender) and also ran sheep on the high part of the summer range that the cattle never used. After shipping time in the fall, Dad turned the sheep back to Andress and then decided he would try to earn his living by running cattle on his ranch. In the spring of 1929, Dad borrowed money on the ranch, on the house in Placerville, and also on a house he had bought from Elmer Walsh in Norwood. With this capital, he purchased one hundred head of white-faced cows. Unfortunately, he would never be a cattle rancher because the great stock market crash hit that year; suddenly the bank was demanding payment on all outstanding mortgages. Dad hadn't had enough time to sell a calf crop or raise money in any other way. Left with no choice, he had to let everything go to satisfy the mortgage. The house in Norwood where Mother lived until shortly before she died in 1988 was saved by selling a homestead Dad owned in Mud Springs Draw. When they were trailing their sheep through there, the sheep outfit of Dan Hughes and John Gonia had always given Dad a hundred dollars a year for the use of the place. John Stokes bought it for six hundred dollars. After moving the family and their belongings from the ranch to Norwood, Dad went to work for the county and hauled gravel on the road with a team and wagon. The wagon belonged to Dad, and the team was borrowed from Howard Davis who had been a good neighbor up on Beaver Mesa. The wagon was loaded and unloaded by hand; dump boards in the bottom of the wagon box helped speed up the unloading process somewhat. The county paid four dollars a day for the man and the team.

Falling back on yet another of his many skills, Dad would put together a crew of sheep shearers in the springtime, without fail. Starting in Texas, the crew worked their way northward to Idaho. They could make the work last several months. On many of these sheep shearing trips, Dad turned the crew westward to

The author at age two with his parents at the ranch.

Seattle, Washington where he could stop for a visit with his daughter, Verna. After leaving there they would sometimes swing down into northern California and shear a few jobs around the area. While passing through northern California in 1932, Dad met a man by the name of Paul Knight. Wanting to come to southwestern Colorado, Mr. Knight offered Dad a twenty-one jewel railroad watch if he would haul him back with the crew. A timber-faller by trade and an excellent ax man, Knight and my oldest brother, Jack, worked together in the woods for several years after that.

In 1933, Dad managed to come up with enough money to buy the Norwood Pool Hall from Bert Combs. In the winter Dad put up ice from the Gurley Reservoir and had cold beer to sell in summer, as well as ice for the numerous ice boxes around town. When electric coolers became available to cool bottled beer, the first one in the town of Norwood was installed by my dad in his pool hall. The need for block ice dwindled after that, and the keg beer sales dropped off. Until failing health forced him to sell out in 1945, Dad kept the pool hall business. Jim and Agatha Dalpez bought the business and its furnishings and moved them to their building which is now the Lone Cone Cafe and Bar. They ran a pool hall in conjunction with the cafe for several years.

My father's ingenuity and his many skills and experiences allowed him to overcome an ever-present instability in the area's job market. Skilled as a cowboy, an entrepreneur, a rancher, and a salesman, Dad often fell back on his skills as a laborer to get the family through hard times.

Chapter 6

THE WOLFE MURDERS

On a spring day toward the end of April, in the year 1926, a local rancher and his young nephew were killed in a cold-blooded fashion for no apparent reason. The killings occurred at the northwest end of the area known as Beaver Mesa; where a lonesome rock chimney now stands, there once was a very nice, two-story house.

The house was built by the old Telluride Mines Company in 1912. The company operated a nearby sawmill where pine and spruce trees were sawed into boards and dimensional timber for the mines. The sawmill hands and log cutters used the house for their lodging place for several years. The house and its surrounding 160 acres was purchased by John Wolfe Sr. around 1920; it was near here that he met with violent death a few years later.

John Wolfe Sr. was about sixty at the time of his murder, and John Wolfe Jr. was about twenty. Old John had a younger brother, Joe, who was the father of John Jr. as well as one other son and two daughters. One of John Jr.'s sisters was held hostage for a short time by the man suspected of the murders; the fact that she was released unharmed is as much a mystery as the murders.

The Wolfe Brothers ran a herd of sheep and owned two different areas of land were the sheep were pastured. The Joe

The Indian sheepherder, George David Nelson, who was thought to be the killer of the Wolfe family.

Wolfe place was located right along the lower beef trail in the upper drainage of Saltado creek at the south end of Beaver Mesa. Just across the beef trail was the cow camp and headquarters of an old-time cowman by the name of Bob Valient. As it was with the house on the John Wolfe property, the only thing that marks the spot where the Joe Wolfe house once stood is a lonely rock chimney; where happy people once lived and raised children is today a stark and solitary place.

The Joe Wolfe place was the location of the summer pasture for the brothers' band of sheep. There was also access to outside land higher up in the mountains. On land owned by the older of the brothers, the spring and fall pasture was five miles below across the mesa in the pines. This range was considerably lower in elevation and had earlier grass in the spring and not so much early snow in the fall. All in all, it was a comfortable set-up; the Wolfe family had a thriving sheep ranching business.

In the spring of 1925, a sheepherder was hired to follow the herds through their migration to the summer pastures. A well-educated Indian man from reservation country to the south, he wore nice clothes and fancy inlaid boots. Young and powerful, his horse was a superb, well-bred animal that had endurance beyond belief. The Indian was an excellent horseman who had the respect of those who had ridden the range with him. It was readily declared that the Indian and his prize horse could cover a hundred miles cross-country in twenty-four hours, if necessary. (Perhaps the next year this claim would be proven true.) The Indian was still employed by the Wolfe Brothers in that fateful spring of 1926.

In late April, the sheep were down in the pines on the early range of the John Wolfe Sr. place. The Indian herder was there tending to them and lambing out the ewes. John Jr. was staying with his uncle to help mend fences, and his older sister had come along with him to do all the cooking. (In the high country, a lot of fence repairing must be done in the spring. Because the early snow freezes to the wires, and then the heavy winter snows pile up on top of that, their combined weight breaks the wires and pulls the staples out of the posts. At times the posts are even broken off and must be replaced as well.)

One day that spring, John Wolfe Sr. and his nephew were found shot to death along a fence line where they had been mending broken wires and repairing the fence. Killed with a high powered rifle, they both were shot in the back. The position of young John's body suggested that he may have turned a little toward the bushwhacker before the fatal bullet struck him down; the unarmed men never even had a chance to defend themselves.

The following account was sobbed out by a hysterical young girl who had walked the five miles from her uncle's house down in the pines to her father's ranch in upper Saltado. She said the Indian sheepherder had stormed into the ranch house after the men left for work that morning and had tied her to a kitchen chair. Leaving the house with a rifle, he rode off in the direction of the fence line that the men had gone to repair. Some time later the Indian returned to the house and set her free. At that point, he told her that he had killed her brother and uncle. Torching the house, he mounted his horse and rode away, never to be heard from again. As rapidly as she could travel afoot the frightened girl headed straight for her home and told about the death of her brother and uncle. A neighbor was immediately dispatched to the town of Placerville to call the sheriff. In the meantime, Joe Wolfe and some of the other men who had gathered at the house took a team and a wagon out to bring the bodies back to the ranch.

Enraged over the senseless murder of the two men, the ranchers on the mesa quickly banded together to try to run down the assassin. Their posse started trailing the Indian's horse from the smouldering ruins of the house to the scene of the killings and back to the house again. Since the murders had not been

George Estep, a man who helped to trail the Indian as far as possible.

witnessed by anyone, no one could prove that the Indian had actually been the one who had done it. In view of the facts, however, it was a sure bet that the sheriff would want to question him about it. The posse worked out his trail to the east rim of Beaver canyon, down to the crossing, and out the other side. When darkness overtook them, the chase had to be abandoned. Bright and early the next morning, the men were back on the trail but had considerable difficulty staying on the tracks because the fugitive who had made the tracks had gone to an awful lot of trouble to make his trail tough to follow. On the second day, the chase was abandoned again. Because the men were so far behind the man they were trailing and the tracks were so difficult to follow, it seemed useless to continue their pursuit. The posse was probably as close to the Indian then as they would ever be. As far as anyone knows, the Indian was never heard of again around there.

Following the Wolfe murders, life on the area sheep ranches was turned upside down for awhile. Worried for their safety, families feared that the Indian sheepherder was hiding out somewhere in the area and that his murder plans may have included more victims than just John Wolfe Sr. and his nephew.

Within just one short month, the posse that had trailed the Indian after the Wolfe murders would be called on to ride this country again. Fearful that the Indian may have kidnapped another victim, a frantic sheep rancher called on these same men. An all-night search followed in an effort to find a lost little boy and his black, curly-haired, bird dog who had strayed too far from home. (See Chapter seven, "Afraid to Answer".)

Twenty-five years later, while Guy Warrick was sheriff of San Miguel County, he heard a rumor about an Indian on the Navajo Reservation; that Indian either knew a great deal about the Wolfe murders or knew someone who did. Mr. Warrick made a trip down to the Indian Agency at Window Rock, Arizona, picked up an Indian, and brought him to Norwood in the hopes that someone could identify him.

Many people around the country had seen the Indian who had worked for the Wolfe Brothers. My father was running sheep at this same time, and our ranches joined the Wolfe property in several places. My older brothers, who did our herding, had visited many times with the Indian herder. They liked him quite well and thought he was a good Indian.

The sheriff's hopes of someone implicating this Indian in the Wolfe Murders were dashed soon after his return to Norwood. If the Indian sheepherder had returned to his reservation, he had probably spent the last twenty-five years losing himself in the vastness of the land and reverting back to his old ways; identification would be virtually impossible after so many years. None who looked at the man with the Sheriff could positively say that it was the same Indian. The Indian I saw with Sheriff Warrick didn't appear to be able to speak or even understand the English language. After a brief stay in Norwood, the Indian was released back to the Navajo Indian Agency. Today, the mystery of the Wolfe Murders remains unsolved.

Chapter 7

AFRAID TO ANSWER

The following tale of a lost little boy and his dog is actually about my brother, Floyd. Born on March 3, 1920, he was six years old the night he was lost (which happened to be on my second birthday, May 31, 1926). With Floyd's kind permission, I have written of his ordeal in the first person. With the accurate memory-work of our late mother, we composed the following account of a night that could have easily ended in tragedy. The fact that it all ended well is proof enough to our family that, as Bryant states in his beautiful "To A Waterfowl," "There is a power whose care, teaches thy way along that pathless coast, the desert and illimitable air. Lone wandering but not lost." The following is Floyd's story.

"It was cold-blooded murder," I can still recall hearing my father say that when those two bodies were found. A senseless and cowardly ambush had taken the lives of two of our neighbors. The victims were an elderly man, who owned a band of sheep with his brother, and his brother's oldest son, John, Jr.

The author's father (seated on a grain binder), Floyd, and Fred Nugent, a neighbor, with his shotgun. This photograph was taken the summer before Floyd was lost overnight.

(See Chapter six, "The Wolfe Murders.") The murderer was believed to be the Indian sheepherder who had hired on with them the year before.

I was six years old the spring that these murders were committed; the talk about the murdering Indian was a daily occurrence. About a month after the killings, I strayed too far from home while out playing with my dog and was lost for a day and a night. My thoughts about the Indian murderer were of very little comfort during that long, lonesome night. The men who took part in the search organized for me were close to me several times during the night, but my fear of the Indian kept me from answering their many calls.

The day I wandered away, my Dad was working a small

A southwest view over the ranch house. In the background are the "Shady Trees" (where Floyd went to play) and Lone Cone.

bunch of ewes and newborn lambs out to the pasture where the rest of the herd was. I was playing with my dog Penny and decided to join Dad and help him drive the sheep. Very gentle, Penny wouldn't hurt a flea but the nervous ewes weren't convinced of this. They were about to stampede out of there and leave their lambs. Dad scolded me about playing around the sheep with the dog and sent me back to the house to play. That was about 10:00 A.M. Little did anyone expect that it would be just about twenty-four hours before the dog or I would be seen again. Although Penny and I started back toward the house, I changed my mind about halfway home and decided we should go to the patch of aspen we called the "Shady Trees" and play there awhile. The grove of trees was about a half-mile southwest of the house and a wonderful place to play.

While I was on the way up to the "Shady Trees," a number of things interrupted my journey. There were rocks to be thrown at birds skimming by and rabbits to be chased through the low brush of the flats. The soft, grassy meadow invited a moment's rest, and I spent time lying on the cool ground and watching the ever-changing cloud patterns overhead. Some of the clouds even took on the shape on an Indian or a bunch of Indians swooping down on some lonely ranch house. I had a vivid imagination. With so many things to see and play pretend with, the expedition to the "Shady Trees" was sidetracked over and over again. By the time the thought of the aspen grove entered my mind again, we had already passed by it, off to the west. A little boy out wandering around the countryside with his dog is surely too engrossed in his wonderful world of play to pay much attention to landmarks of any kind or to the time. By this point, we had traveled over a rise in the ground to a point where nothing familiar was visible in any direction. Because I was sure I hadn't gone quite far enough, Penny and I took off in earnest to reach the grove and play before Mother called us in for lunch.

We must have traveled close to two miles west across the mesa to the rim of Beaver Canyon and at least a half-mile down to the bottom where Beaver Creek runs. At that time of year the creek was a wild, raging torrent. Completely flowing out of its banks, it swept along at a terrific pace toward its confluence with the San Miguel River. These icy waters and deep undertows meant sure death to anyone who might fall in. Even a powerful swimmer such as a horse would be no match for the fury of this mountain stream when in full flood. The highest water always came down in the night; here I stood, along the banks of such a mighty torrent, with darkness falling fast . . . and I was lost.

I later told my parents that when I thought about crossing the creek, I first held a stick out into the current to test it. The swiftness of the water jerked the stick out of my hand with such force that it made a lasting impression. Mother had told me many time to always check the force of a stream this way. If the water jerked the stick out of my hand, I was not to try to cross even with a horse. Since Penny sensed the danger and kept whimpering and crowding in between me and the water to keep me away from the banks, there was little chance of me putting even my big toe in the water.

As darkness settled in, I started back up the hill to find a place that didn't look quite so dark and foreboding as the bottom of the canyon. About halfway up, my small body started feeling the effects of the long hike and the climb in and out of this steep canyon. Although I needed rest and nourishment because I hadn't eaten anything since early morning, I knew there wasn't much prospect of finding anything to eat. When I did lie down to rest, I soon fell fast asleep.

At approximately the time I reached the bottom of the canyon, Mother had realized that I hadn't come back to the house for lunch. She found out from Dad that I had not been with him either. When he came in to eat at 2:00 P.M., he told Mother then that he had sent me back to the house to play nearly four hours earlier. The immediate area around the ranch was searched thoroughly as was the "Shady Trees" area. By 4:00 P.M., Dad had organized a group of the neighbors to help with the search. There were men in the search party who could trail a termite across a tombstone, but it took all the skill they had to follow the meandering trail of a little boy and his dog. The men picked up my trail with the tracks of the dog alongside and followed them down to the bottom of the canyon. There, they

Eli Kell, a neighbor across Beaver Canyon, who helped in the all night search for Floyd and the dog. Note that most people carried guns on their saddles.

spotted our tracks in numerous places along the bank of the treacherous mountain stream. When darkness fell solid, the posse broke up into small groups and searched the brush and rocky hillside all night. Periodically through the night the groups of men met to build a fire, discuss the places where they had already searched, and to consider further search plans.

During one of the meeting sessions, while the men stood around a campfire, I was awakened by the whining and restlessness of the dog. Cold and hungry, I raised myself up to look around. Repeatedly the men called out for me and the dog. Because he had been used by them to hunt grouse and prairie chickens, Penny knew this group well and would have gone to any one of them if I had not been holding my ground. My wild imagination got in the way of my good sense. *I wasn't gonna be killed by that Indian.* Every time someone would call the dog, he would start to go to them. When I wouldn't go too, he would come back and stay with me. I really thought they were a bunch of Indians who wanted to find me and kill me the way they had killed our neighbors. Less than a quarter of a mile separated me from the worried men, but I was too afraid to answer. As we moved farther on up the hill, I found an old rotted out pine log that had blown full of oak leaves. It was here that Penny and I spent the remainder of the night—curled up together and covered with leaves to stay warm.

Mother worked like mad to help out with the search. She fixed lunches for the search party and sent the food out to them by a neighbor who knew where to find them. Over and over she left the house and walked a half mile or so to call out for me and the dog. She would listen for any encouraging sounds, like the click of horse hooves coming along the rocky trails. When no response came, she would go back to the house and try to busy herself with housework until she could no longer stand the strain and the worry. Then she would go out once again and do her calling and listening. There was no doubt that Mother was plenty worried. If she had had any knowledge that my meandering had taken me down into Beaver Canyon and close to those raging flood waters, she would not have spent the hours worrying at the house. Without any doubts whatsoever, she would have been among the searchers combing that brush and rock-strewn canyonside.

Sometime after midnight, a neighbor lady drove over in her spring wagon to keep Mother company. The two women sat and talked for awhile, but soon both went outside and walked away from the house to call for me and listen once again for sounds of returning horsemen. The long night passed slowly as the women spent the hours calling and listening . . . waiting and praying.

Because the search party hadn't been able to pick up my trail as it left the bank of the stream, many of the men, including my father, feared that I might have fallen into the stream. On the other hand, their good sense told them that if this had been my fate, surely my dog would be somewhere around here or would have returned to the ranch. The men couldn't shake the dreadful feeling, however. Since I was instructed never to wander this far from the ranch house, they had to suspect that both the dog and I had met with an ill fate.

Dad said they would search the rest of the night; if I wasn't found by daylight, he would ride the fifteen miles into Norwood and get another party of men together. His plan was to put a seine at the mouth of Beaver Creek where it empties into the San Miguel River, in case the dog and I had been swept away in the creek and drowned.

Daylight came, and there was still no sign of the dog or me. After giving last minute instructions to the searchers, Dad headed his weary horse toward the Beef Trail Crossing and the road to Norwood. With a lump in his throat and an ache in his heart, he stopped for just one more look around and one last holler. His deep voice had scarcely stopped echoing between the high rims of the canyon when it awakened me. I recognized my father's voice, as did Penny, and I was no longer afraid to answer. Besides, I could no longer contain the eager dog. Together we came bounding out of the brush not fifty feet from where my father stood. It was a most joyous reunion, and Dad held me close for a long, long time. Penny was beside himself

The author's father with Penny, waiting to flush the prairie chickens which were plentiful then.

with excitement, and Dad gave him some grateful, affectionate pats. When it was obvious that all was well, Dad asked me if I had gotten cold. "I was cold for a little while," I replied with wide-eyed excitement, "but when I saw those Indians down by the fire, Penny and I climbed up the hill a ways and found a big old log that had a lot of leaves in it. We crawled in there and covered up with them and stayed warm all night!" Dad couldn't help but chuckle at my imagination and offered me a sandwich he had been saving, just in case I was found. Since it had been close to twenty-four hours since I had last eaten, Dad knew I was plenty hungry. Dad mounted his horse and lifted me up behind the saddle; off we rode to join the rest of the search party. It would have been hard to find a more relieved and happy group of men.

At daylight, Mother could stand no more of the waiting and worrying. She went out to the corral, caught one of Dad's horses, saddled him up, and rode off in the direction that the search party had taken the afternoon before. After riding four or five miles down toward the pines, she didn't see any fresh tracks, so she swung west along a trail that would have eventually taken her to the Beef Trail Crossing. After about a mile of riding along this trail, she suddenly noticed the tracks of quite a few horses that had recently come up out of Beaver Canyon. The tracks were heading straight back to the ranch. From the way the ground was torn up, she could tell that the horsemen were pushing their mounts pretty hard. Mother knew it had to be the returning search party bringing some kind of urgent word about her little boy. Good news or bad, she knew she must return home. With a lift of the reins she urged the horse into a long, easy run—eating up the miles back to the ranch.

When Mother rode in, most of the neighbors had already left for their homes. I was playing out in the yard, and Penny was dozing in the sun by the porch. What a wonderful sight for a worried mother! After she ran up to me, she held me close for a long time in the same relieved way that Dad had done earlier. Completely exhausted both mentally and physically from the all-night search and the strain of worrying about me, Dad had already gone to bed. Mother looked me over real well and saw

Results of the hunt—fried chicken for supper.

that I was fine. She saw no tear streaks or smudges on my face where a soiled little hand might have wiped away some tears. In fact, my nonchalance about the whole episode set the tone for the rest of the family to get on with another day of ranch life.

Chapter 8

THE STRAWBERRY ROAN OF 1948

1947 was the year that my dad died. As I look back now, there was probably no greater tribute to his memory than the fact that I took a job breaking horses on the Hughes Ranch in Dry Creek Basin that same year. I was the same age then that my dad had been when he started breaking horses for a living over on the Dew Drop and Billy Creek ranges.

When I was working at the nearby Whatley Brothers ranch, Ed Netherton, who was the foreman for Dan Hughes, had talked to me several times about coming down to the headquarters ranch and going to work on a string of green horses. They had about twenty-five in the string; it was a job which could last all winter. Although I had already contracted to guide deer hunters that fall and had made tentative plans to go to Arizona for the winter, I was really interested in the work. I told Ed if I decided to take the job I would be there by early November.

Soon after deer season was over, I arrived at the Hughes Ranch ready for work. The following morning just about everyone who could get on a horse did so and helped round up the horse herd. The biggest percentage of the herd were four and five year-olds who hadn't had a hand on them since they were weaned and branded. Their behavior was not very much different from that of a bunch of wild horses. As a matter of fact, they were wild in most every way; their roaming, however, had been within the confines of a fenced range.

Two animals in the bunch immediately caught my eye. Both were red roans but one was a much darker red; I would call it a strawberry roan. Neither one would have won any prizes unless it would be for being ugly. Later I would discover their dispositions matched their appearance. Right away I pegged the lighter colored roan as a mate for another horse I knew; the two would make a good wagon team. The sheep camp wagon had to be moved from the winter range, and there was a need for a team and wagon in areas like North Mountain and Beaver Park in the summer months.

Ed and I and some of the ranch hands cut out from the herd a black mare, a sorrel mare, a bay gelding, and the eye-catching strawberry roan. We all marveled at the roan's spirited gate around the slippery, muddy corral. In the wet spots where most of the other frantic horses had slipped and gone down, he was never off of his feet. Running around while the rest of the herd was milling around nervously or bumping into the corral fence and one another, he was absolutely as cat-like as anything I had ever seen. He rolled snorts out his nostrils at every breath. I thought then, *If this horse ever breaks, he is sure going to make a good mount for somebody.*

As you might expect, I broke the Strawberry Roan first. The next few broke easily, and I turned them over to the sheep camp. In addition, I had nine of the others pretty well along when winter hit with a vengeance. After a week of hard snowing and wind, all of the roads were closed; travel was impossible.

The first night after the storm cleared off, the thermometer plunged to thirty-three degrees below zero, and the ranch hands in the bunkhouse nearly froze to death. Ed came out to get us at about 4:30 A.M. to help him get equipment started so the feeding could be done. He opened the bunkhouse door and stomped his feet to shake away the cold. "There ain't a damn thing between here and the North Pole but a two-wire fence and most of it is down," he grumbled. We talked Ed into building a fire first, so we could all get thawed out a little. Once warmed up, we headed out to see what the storm had delivered.

My corrals were an absolute mess—frozen rock hard and so lumpy from tracks that they couldn't be used for anything. It was difficult to even walk across them. All of my ropes and gear were frozen and useless. I told Ed, "Why fight it? I'll come back in the spring and finish up with the horses then." I knew of some horses down in Disappointment Valley that needed breaking, and the weather down there was a little more forgiving.

A local rancher, Francis Hardman, decided to give every returning World War II Veteran in the area a horse of breaking age. I hadn't heard of any of the horses actually being broke as yet, so I saddled up the Strawberry Roan and rode down to Cedar to see about breaking the first of these gifts. I stayed two weeks with Bud and Norma McCall until I had broken one horse for them. Because he couldn't be left without riding for more than a day or two, I continued working on the roan.

After this, I rode a few miles up Disappointment Creek and broke a horse for Alvin Satley. His brother-in-law, Don Royce, decided he wanted me to break the grey horse Francis had given to him. Since things had been going very smoothly for awhile, (both with my own horse and the easy time I had with the McCall's horse), I was not too surprised when I found the grey horse was difficult, to say the least. He was eight years old and more than a little spoiled. If I hadn't had so much practice riding the bucking roan every day, I might have given up on the grey

76

horse. Finally giving in first, he broke in just fine, so I turned him over to Don and headed on up the creek to the ranch of Neil Bankston. Neil had never seen my roan horse before. At his first glance, I could tell he was skeptical. Roman-headed and narrow between the eyes (which accounted for most of his ugliness) the animal was also a little "creasefallen" in front of his withers. His rather prominent hip bones made his hind quarters resemble those of a house cat. (An old cowboy expression is "cat ham'd".) After a long winter of riding, he was also somewhat leggy and slim-bodied. Neil just couldn't hold back. "Son, that horse will never amount to a damn. I can tell he's a one-man horse and about half outlaw along with it. You'd better watch him all the time." I knew all this full well by now, for I had been riding that unpredictable "cayuse" for better than five months!

The Strawberry Roan of 1948 after nearly a year of riding.

77

From conversations with the old-time cowboys that I knew (Don Loveridge, Kip Woods, and Fred Sharp) and from the stories of Baley Hurd, I learned there was a consensus of opinion about horses that had a demeanor and appearance similar to that of my roan. Because the old cowboys' advice had been passed on to me so many times, I was quite familiar with what to expect from horses with certain looks about them. A song I had heard many years before, could have easily been written about this horse. Called "The Strawberry Roan," the song had a most appropriate verse that goes like this, "He was ewe-necked and old, and narrow at the jaw, you could tell with one eye, he's a regular outlaw."

In mid-April of 1948, I left the Bankston place on the roan and went back to Dry Creek Basin and the Hughes Ranch. Ed Netherton didn't have any corrals to spare for breaking horses, though, so I continued on up to the Whatley Ranch and found work there. I kept the roan with me as I knew for certain he was not yet ready for general ranch riding. That first day on the ranch, I had commented about what a good mount he would make for somebody. I had no idea that somebody would be me and only me; the roan turned out to be a one-man horse. Since I was the only person that had ever laid a hand on him during the first eight months after he was broke, I was the one man he trusted. He would not tolerate strangers. If anyone but me tried to catch him, he would run around the corral blowing snorts the way he had done that first day I laid eyes on him. If he got cornered somehow, he would just sort of settle back on his hindquarters and roll snorts until a fellow was just plain afraid to walk any closer. It never was clear whether he was going to just stampede over the top of you or eat you alive.

For two months in the spring, May through June, the Lilylands Canal (See Chapter nineteen, "The Lilylands Development Company.") that supplies the irrigation water for Dry Creek Basin had to be monitored thoroughly. Every inch of the thirty-seven mile long canal had to be checked out for eroding banks, low spots, debris, etc. to ensure that the irrigation water flowed smoothly. Nowadays, jeeps and pickups can travel all of the ditch bank, but in 1948 it was a long, hard ride—hard on the rider and hard on the horse. The ditch rider carried a shovel and a half dozen gunny sacks tied behind the saddle. To make the trip in good time, almost all of the riding had to be done at a long trot. If a low place on the bank was spotted, where the canal might wash out, the rider would stop and hobble his horse. A sack or two would be filled with dirt and rolled into place. With a few sod chunks placed just so and a little tromping, the repair was made. This routine was repeated all the way up the canal to the headgate where horse and rider could finally rest for an hour or so and eat lunch. Then, it was time to saddle up and head back down the canal bank to the ranch. (The round trip was usually done in about twelve or thirteen hours.) Several good men with sound horses in the Basin took their turn at making the ride. My roan horse was five years old that spring, and I made the trip up the canal and back on him several times.

Coming into the ranch, many horses used for the canal ride would buck their rider off if he tried anything funny. My horse was no exception to this. No amount of riding seemed to take his spirit away, and he grew to be as tough as rawhide. The end of the day always found him bright-eyed, ears alert, and stepping along quite spritely. Since that time I have often wished for a horse like him to enter in today's endurance races.

In July of 1948, I received a letter from my brother, Floyd, in Rifle. He informed me that I could go to work for the Bureau of Mines if I cared to come up there. After I thought about it for awhile, I decided that I would like a change. Since it meant a lot more money than what I could scrape together by breaking half-wild horses, I put a new set of shoes on the roan and took him back to the Hughes Ranch. After riding him for eight months, I could do anything on him I had ever tried. I had roped cattle in the corral and pulled firewood along behind him for branding fires. With me he was plumb gentle; well, maybe he was a little kicky and not to be trusted too far, but, for the most part, he behaved himself.

Ed Netherton turned the roan over to an ex-bronc rider who was working at the ranch. One day, he and the roan started on a ride for Beaver Park. The old bronc rider was bucked off twice before they were half way there. Humiliated by this, he made sure that he would not be bucked off again. Walking to a nearby sheep camp, he borrowed the herder's horse and led the roan the rest of the way to Beaver Park. The roan promptly got a reputation as a bucker and an outlaw and became almost impossible to catch. He was brought back to the ranch and kept penned up all winter.

While the roan was making a name for himself at the Hughes Ranch, I finished up my work in Rifle and prepared to go to Arizona for the winter. Once in Arizona, a cowboy named Dick Weining and I teamed up to work on a big horse ranch near Tucson. During that winter, we broke about a hundred horses. The job went well, and we finished up just as the really hot weather was moving in.

When I left Arizona early that summer, I went back to Dry Creek Basin, Colorado and headed straight for the Hughes Ranch. I felt certain they would have work for me by now. When I arrived at the Ranch, I found that Ed Netherton had left. Another man I knew quite well, Dean Fields, had taken his place. Dean and I struck up a conversation; before long, he pointed toward the corrals and asked me if I knew anything about the roan horse out there. When I said I might, we started up there to take a look. I didn't have to get too much closer to recognize the horse. He was the same roan that I had broken almost a year and a half earlier. He was fat and sleek as a mole and a perfect Strawberry Roan color. Dean didn't know what to do with him. He couldn't get anybody to ride the horse, and he

The author on one of the many colts that he "broke" during the summer of 1949.

was extremely hard to catch. I told Dean that I had been the one to break the horse and that I had spent eight months using him for various tasks. All the time I was talking to Dean I kept glancing over at the horse. I couldn't help but notice the way he looked at me and listened to my voice. When I asked Dean if they had a halter handy, he sent his younger brother into a shed. Returning with a workhorse halter that had about fifteen feet of half-inch, softwist rope tied to it, he handed it to me, and I walked out into the corral. I wasn't certain what was going to happen, but I had a strong feeling that the roan knew me and still trusted me. I had nothing with me that would entice the horse: no oat bucket, no sugar lumps, no carrots—just me and the halter. As if I were greeting an old friend, I continued talking and walking slowly, while keeping my voice steady.

By the time I took four or five more steps, I swear I saw the light of recognition come into his eyes. His whole manner seemed to change, and I was able to get close to him. Although he snorted a few times, I knew him too well to be bothered by those ferocious, rolling sounds. After patting his neck a little, I playfully scratched him under his jawbone. Then, I slowly slid the halter on him and led him to where Dean and his brother stood in utter disbelief. Introducing the horse as my old friend, I led him around the corral a few times and stopped in the middle. When I coiled up the rope in my left hand, I let the coils hang on my arm; then I reached up and got a handful of his mane and swung up on his bare back. Not a single cowboy around the Hughes outfit had been able to ride the roan with a saddle on his back; here I was sitting on him bareback with nothing but a halter to handle him with. Urging him to move out, we went around the corral several times in both directions. Then I eased him into a trot, and we trotted and loped around the corral a few more times before stopping in front of Dean and his brother, who were still standing there in shock. Dean finally said, "There isn't a thing wrong with that horse. These guys around here are just afraid of him. I'll get somebody to get some use out of him."

Dean was unable to get anyone to take the horse that summer. Late that fall, Calvin Ficklin, a friend of mine said he would like to use the roan in Hamm Canyon, to pack bags of sheep pellets during the winter. Calvin really liked the roan, and the horse seemed to tolerate him better than most people. Calvin never had to catch him though. In sheep camp, the horses were always tied out to a cedar tree.

When winter came, Calvin started out the first day by loading the roan up with two sacks of pellets (one hundred pounds each). About fifty yards out from the camp, the roan went into a fit of bucking and scattered the two sacks of pellets all over the head of Hamm Canyon. Taking him back to camp, Calvin loaded three sacks on the horse and started out again. He didn't get much farther that time before the 'ole Strawberry Roan broke in two again and scattered the three sacks of pellets. Now, Calvin was a very patient man. Undaunted by the horse's stubbornness, he turned the roan back to camp again. This time, he loaded him with four sacks of pellets and started out again. When they had gone about as far as the roan could tolerate (which was about as far as they had made it the two times before), he lowered his head and tried with all his might to buck again. All he could do was to moan and groan and hump up his back; he couldn't get his feet to leave the ground. Calvin had managed to outsmart the roan. From that day forward, all winter long, Calvin packed him with four sacks of pellets for scattered bands of sheep in the Hamm Canyon and Bull Canyon areas.

As romantic and pleasant as it would be to close on a happy note, there is, unfortunately, a very sad and pitiable ending to this story. The old roan horse didn't retire to a nice ranch somewhere to live out his days in green pastures in the summer and a warm barn full of hay in the winter. He never grew old and became that special horse who gave all the neighbor kids their first ride. One night, in March of 1952, he managed to slip out of his halter and ate a half sack of wheat-alfalfa pellets. He was dead from protein poisoning (a type of founder) before the sun went down the next day.

Chapter 9

THE PINTO GRIZZLY

The Legend of the Lone Cone

The first sighting of the Pinto Grizzly took place over in Disappointment Valley in 1893. An old female grizzly bear with two cubs was spotted in the mouth of a small, rough canyon that drained from the foothills of North Mountain out into the valley.

Henry Knight, who had taken up a Homestead there in 1882, first saw the bears. Since he had livestock close by, he set a pack of dogs onto them and ran them clear to the top of North Mountain. One of the grizzly cubs was quite different from the other; he was much larger, and each of his flanks had a large, distinctive, patch of white that nearly reached up to his back.

Where the bears had come from, no one could guess. The mother bear and the small cub where never spotted again. When it was a yearling, the larger, male pinto cub was spotted the following summer on the north side of the Lone Cone. Alfred Dunham and Mel Turner were riding after cattle and looking over the range when they spotted the Pinto Grizzly. "That ain't no ordinary bear," remarked Dunham. "Just look at those big patches of white in the flanks."

"Yeh, they almost meet on top of the back," added Turner, "and he sure 'nuff ain't no ordinary bear. We're looking at about a year-old grizzly and a pinto at that. Who would have supposed there'd be a grizzly bear over in this area?" To get a look at a grizzly bear was a rare treat and certainly topped off the day's events.

In the evenings around the bunkhouses, the subject of the Pinto Grizzly cub would be brought up and discussed many times. No one there had ever seen one, and none of them knew anyone who had. The Pinto cub was definitely out of grizzly country, but it appeared he intended to make this area his home.

Several years passed without many sightings of the Pinto Grizzly; most people thought he had just moved on. Infrequent as they were, the sightings revealed that the bear was growing up. Although he hadn't done much to advertise his presence, a few more years would change that. The need for nourishment for his thousand pound body and the storing up of fat for the long winter hibernations would cause him to become ever more visible around the countryside.

About 1895 when William Souther and James Nix were running a trap line in the upper drainage of Disappointment Valley, they had an encounter with a huge bear. They were almost at the head of West Naturita Creek in the pass between the Lone Cone and North Mountain when the incident with the grizzly took place. Nix shot the bear with his repeating rifle. Badly wounded, the bear charged the men. Although Nix emptied his rifle into the chest area of the charging animal, the beast kept on coming. Souther raised his old single-shot carbine and dropped the bear right at their feet. It was a large female grizzly; the bear's skull measured eighteen inches, ear to ear. They thought that this huge bear was probably the mother of the Pinto Grizzly that was ranging in the Lone Cone area.

Around the turn of the century, stockmen running cattle on

the Lone Cone and other nearby ranges began finding carcasses of cattle which had been partly eaten and dragged away. The sign around the kills was unmistakably that of a grizzly. What other animal would leave tracks fifteen inches long and eight

Cowboys in 1884: Bill Hamilton and his crew, ready to go to a Lone Cone roundup. (Courtesy of the Colorado Historical Society.)

inches wide, with claw marks touching the ground three inches in front of the toes? Very few other types of bears could drag 500 or more pounds of partially eaten cow carcass back into the rough and down-timber places where these were found. There was sure enough a cattle-killing grizzly in the country now. He would have to be killed at the first opportunity. An old cattleman from Dry Creek Basin known as "Bood" Moore, said it all when he remarked that every cowboy who made the beef ride on the Cone had better be packing a Winchester.

The Pinto Grizzly ranged over the Lone Cone and Beaver Park area but he had been known (by his kills) to have been on North Mountain, the head of Plateau Creek, and also in the

Groundhog Divide country. Covering about thirty square miles of country, he was the only grizzly in that whole area and he went just about wherever he pleased. Years would go by without any trace of the bear. Then, out of the blue, some cowboy would come across the remains of a cow that showed all the signs of a grizzly kill, and everyone would know the Pinto bear was still around.

At all the roundups on the Lone Cone, the cowboys packed their guns; each one hoping to be the one to get a shot at the legendary Pinto Grizzly. The long-awaited opportunity came in the fall of 1915. Getting old and having more difficulty making kills, the bear was more inclined to "locate" (stay around a certain area) and not travel as much. When time runs out for an old bear, it usually runs out in a hurry. Such was the case for the Pinto Grizzly. Jumped early one morning while feeding on a dead cow, he was chased by cowboys. After running most of the morning, he quit the north slope of the Cone and headed for the rough canyon country across Goshorn Flat toward the east. Out in the open in the big flats, the old bear made a fatal mistake. Two men, who had been notified by a cowboy who quit the chase to go for more help, were cutting across the flat on horseback. Now they had the bear in sight.

When the men got close enough to start shooting, they both began firing their rifles at the bear: Indian Henry with a 30-30 Winchester and a government trapper named Sim Galloway with a 30-40 Krag. Before the old bear went down for good, he had been hit several times by each of the men. The bullets from the 30-30 didn't penetrate into any vital areas. They had mushroomed in his hair and fat and were so matted with both, they hardly looked like bullets at all. The heavier, more powerful bullets from the 30-40 Krag did penetrate some vital areas, and several passed through the lungs, thus causing the death of the big bear.

When Dick Dunham (son of Alfred) saw the hide of the

Pinto Grizzly, he remarked that his dad had seen the animal on the Lone Cone when it was a yearling cub—twenty-two years earlier. The hide of the great Pinto Grizzly completely covered a wagon box.

Chapter 10

BALEY HURD

There Never Was a Cowboy That Couldn't Be Throwed, or a Horse That Couldn't Be Rode

Baley Hurd was my uncle. He was also a cowboy who lived a rather wild and reckless life between the years 1900–1921. The facts of his life and the events that pertained to his life are presented here in the most accurate and honest manner possible. Inquiring, examining, and sifting through the abundance of tall tales about Baley's life left me with a difficult story to present in a factual manner. To portray the man's life accurately meant looking into a few sealed closets and rattling a few skeletons. In fact, this account may rattle a few people who are alive today. Ways were different back in the days when Baley was at his prime; people had their own way of settling things. There is no intent on my part (expressed or implied) to harm anyone's reputation.

Baley wasn't a gun-totin' bad man. He was actually two people in the same body: the drunk Baley Hurd and the sober

one. They were as different as sunlight and shadow. When he was on a drinking spree, he *was* a bully and a bigot. Tough and mean around men, he was oh, so sweet and gentle with the ladies. When he picked fights, he usually picked on the toughest men he could find. Sometimes he tangled with lesser men, but it was usually because they picked a fight with him for what they could get out of it. Although Baley Hurd was not the best family man of that era either, he had a lot of company in that category. An exceedingly good neighbor, he was very well liked by almost everyone who knew him. Because of the nature of his work, a lot of his neighbors didn't get to know him very well. Riding broncs, breaking mean and spoiled horses, and punchin' cows for some big cow outfits kept him away from home an awful lot of the time.

Born in Sawpit, Colorado around the year 1885, Baley Hurd was the second son of a family of four boys and one girl. His childhood was mostly spent riding the miners' burros that were turned loose to graze in the hills around Sawpit, Vanadium, and Placerville country. To support the family, his mother took in washing and cooked meals for the boarders who worked in the mines around there. Baley's father was a no-account Georgia hillbilly who didn't care for people or towns. He lived out in the hills much of the time. With just a gun, his horse, and a bed, he lived off the land like an Indian and never bothered anyone. Once a month or so he would come home for clothes and clean blankets. After staying a few days, he'd be gone again. I'm sure he was no influence on Baley, one way or the other.

As Baley grew older he became a very good hand at breaking horses. He had learned to be an excellent rider and was seldom thrown from a bucking horse. Baley always rode his horses "clean"; there were no gimmicks to foul a horse. Many cowboys had the reputation of being bad medicine for a mean bronc, but they gained their reputations not for their skill in breaking a horse, but in the ways they would foul a horse and take a big advantage. Some would tie up a front leg, i.e. bend it at the knee, and then with the bottom of the hoof up, tie it to the saddle horn with a short piece of rope. Then they would mount the horse and ride until it was lathered with sweat and staggering from weakness before they would let the foot go to the ground. This could usually be done without even having to dismount. Others would hobble (tie) their stirrups to the front cinch and wedge their body in the saddle with a bucking roll. Baley Hurd never did use any of these tactics. Making his reputation riding horses naturally and letting them do their best, he always did plenty of work for local cattlemen who appreciated his way with horses. Baley learned to be a good cowboy as well and handled his share of the cow-work while riding a bronc. This work took him all over the country, and he made friends everywhere he worked.

Being raised up in the mining camps the way he had been, Baley learned a lot about fighting and how to protect himself. After he matured, he was a very powerful man with tremendous arms and shoulders; thick around the waist, he was slim in the hips and legs. Hard years of riding broncs had made him pure bone and muscle. He was a cowboy's cowboy, a fighter's fighter, and a pretty fair hand with the ladies. He truly became a legend in his time.

In 1906, Baley met and married my aunt, Mamie Beach. She was born and raised on California Mesa near Delta. After obtaining the necessary education, she was awarded a teaching certificate and took a job teaching at the Leopard Creek School that same year. She and Baley lived around Placerville, Colorado and that vicinity until 1911. In the summer of 1906 when Baley Hurd was married, there was a big Fourth of July celebration at the old log schoolhouse on Hastings Mesa. Everyone from miles around attended, including people from Deep Creek

Mesa to the southeast and Ironsprings Mesa across Leopard Creek to the northwest. Also, all the residents from along Leopard Creek at the top of Dallas Divide all the way down to Placerville made their way to the festivities. After the picnic was over, the dance would begin; this was a big celebration. Since no one wanted to start home in the dark, they danced all night. With the sunrise, they would eat the left-overs from the picnic and head for home.

My mother's parents, Elias and Ella Beach and his brother Will and his wife, Ida, had homesteaded in Horsefly Park on a couple of quarter sections. Accompanied by all of their children, they would take part in these Fourth of July shindigs. During the picnic the kids would play all kinds of games, and the women would typically sit and talk, sew, and cook. The men gathered for games of horseshoes and shooting at targets for prizes. Usually, someone had a jug or two of moonshine whiskey, and everyone enjoyed a few sociable drinks. Whiskey seems to have a bad effect on certain people. After a few drinks, they start hunting trouble and wanting to fight. On this particular day, before the afternoon had really even got rolling, Jonce Collins and Baley Hurd were into a fight. They fought around an hour or so; neither one was getting the best of the other. Both men were bleeding from numerous places, but they didn't quit. Finally, Baley's pure brute strength and endurance stood him in good stead, and he started getting the better of the exchanges. At this point, Jonce Collins picked up a piece of stove wood and started beating Baley with it. Not to be outdone any, Baley picked up a chunk, too. They both beat on each other until Jonce went to the ground and was unable to get up. Collin's sister, who was there from Telluride with a buggy, took care of washing and bathing his wounds. With help, she loaded him into the buggy and took him home.

In 1911, Baley went to work for Earnest Maupin and his brother, who were running cattle on the Roubideau side of

Uncompaghre Plateau. They lived down there that year; Baley punched cows and broke horses and Mamie taught at the little country school where Roubideau Creek flows into the Gunnison River. While they were living on the Roubideau, Baley's father

This sign is near the old one room schoolhouse where Mamie Hurd taught in the year 1911.

came for a visit and died while he was there. As was his wish, he was buried up on a hill in a grove of cedars away from the ranch and far from any town.

Before they left the Roubideau in 1912, Baley and Mamie's first child was born, and she was named Arvilla. (She is presently living in Denver, Colorado.) Even after they moved most of their operation to the south side of the Uncompaghre to an area known as Tabeguache Basin, Baley continued working for the Maupin Brothers. Baley moved his family to nearby Nucla, Colorado where they lived for the next three years. During this period of time, two more children were born. Sadly, both of these children died during the next four years. The girl, Wilma Lyle, whom they called "Sissy," choked to death on a button. The boy, Emmett, died during the terrible flu epidemic of 1918.

In the fall of 1913, Baley and his family took some time off from the ranch and went to Placerville to spend a month or so visiting friends and relatives. Baley had three brothers and a sister living nearby, so they had a lot of talking to catch up on. Also, Baley had a female acquaintance who lived up on Leopard Creek above the hamlet of Leonard, Colorado. Leonard was the name of a big cattle outfit that had its headquarters down in Unaweep Valley. Called the Leonard or Lenard Cattle Company, its summer range included nearly all of the Uncompaghre Plateau. At the time that Uncompaghre was being used by the Leonard Cattle Company, it was called Leonard Mesa. They also had a summer headquarters on Leopard Creek. Shortly after 1900, the families living there had enough children to warrant a school, and it was naturally called the Leonard School House. By the time I was a small child, a community had evolved there. In the later years, most people knew the place as Green Mountain Lodge because someone had built a number of small cabins there in the hope of attracting tourists and sportsmen.

In spite of his love for his wife and children, Baley still wanted to see this woman. She was one of the Curry girls; I believe the one who merited Baley Hurd's attention was named Alice.

When word got around that there was to be a masquerade dance at the Frank Graves Dance hall in Placerville on Halloween, just about everyone in the whole area made plans to attend. Baley and Alice Curry decided that the only way they could go to the dance together would be for her to go dressed as a man and for Baley to go dressed as a woman. He was a natural for this because he loved a practical joke. Later in the evening, Baley made his way over to a group of women and sat down. Just at that moment, they were wondering where Baley Hurd was and why he wasn't at the dance. The talk about Baley gradually drifted around to the subject of infidelity and what a low-down skunk he was for stepping around with the ladies and for treating Mamie so shamefully. It didn't take Baley long to get a belly-full of that conversation. Jumping out into the middle of the dance floor, he lifted the long dress high enough to show his men's clothing underneath and a six-shooter sticking out of his waistband. Pulling out the gun, he shot out all the lights in the dance hall, grabbed up his masqueraded date, and disappeared into the night. The dance hall emptied out immediately; everyone ran to hide someplace for fear there would be more shooting. My mother, Mamie Hurd's sister, was at the dance that night. While she was running for safety up a hillside behind the dance hall, she sprained her ankle quite badly and had to have Bill Cassity and another young man help her home. Once the dance broke up, the evening was ruined for quite a few people, particularly one young lady who emerged from the frightened crowd to unhappily discover the litter of yellow and black crepe paper that had once been the wings of her magnificent butterfly costume.

After the incident of shooting out the lights at the dance hall, Baley came home to his family and patched things up with Mamie. Returning to Nucla, Baley continued his employment with Ern Maupin. During the three years that Baley was working for the Maupins, they took in a lot of horses to break and stayed busy with the cattle—branding, roping and moving them about the range. This work was the best way to break young horses into cow work. With extensive range to ride over on the Roubideau as well as in Tabegauche, it took a lot of horses to do

Baley Hurd in 1918.

the work; Baley never tired of breaking them. Baley and Ern Maupin camped together hundreds of times and in hundreds of places. Ern said that he had never once seen Baley Hurd with a gun; he'd never seen one in his bedroll or war-bag. Until the incident at the dance hall, he didn't know he even owned one. In fact, Ern said that if there was one thing that Baley was afraid of, it was a gun. Maupin knew that the brute physical strength Baley possessed was all that he needed to settle an argument with any of the local roughnecks who occasionally got primed up on rotgut whiskey and wanted to try him out. Since Baley could take the fight out of a raw range bronc just as easy, this was the kind of work he liked the best. His reputation as a bronc rider and all-around hand with horses never seemed to quit growing. It far outshone any reputation he had with a gun.

In 1917, Baley left the employment of the Maupin Ranch and moved back to Placerville, where he took a job running a saloon and doing some of the bartending. Pregnant with their last child, Mamie gave birth to a girl whom they named Lois in September of 1918. (Lois Hurd is now Mrs. Chester Haptonstall and lives with her husband on Garnet Mesa near Delta, Colorado.) Most of the whiskey sold in the saloons those days was local product (moonshine), and the saloon keepers were ever on the look-out for new suppliers and better products. The moonshiners' stills were regularly busted up and burned. Getting a line on a still somewhere, revenue agents would raid it, dumping out all the mash and whiskey, and damage the still so it could never be used again.

Placerville, Colorado, at this time, was the largest shipping point for cattle in Colorado and the second largest in the United States. There were always a lot of cowboys and cowmen drifting in and out of the saloons while they were in town waiting for their cattle to ship. One day, while talking to some cowboys from Disappointment Valley, Baley found out, in strictest confidence, that he could get all the whiskey his bar could ever use from over there. He also learned he could find a place to make his own moonshine. Given the opportunity for operation, Baley quickly decided to give it a try.

Moving his family to the community of Cedar, he found employment with an old cattleman named Joe Bankston. Taking the job of school-teacher as she usually did, Mamie Hurd proved to be an excellent "all grades" teacher who was in demand wherever she happened to be.

Before too much time had passed, Baley got himself into yet another fight, due to his drunkenness. This time he came very close to losing his life. Quite drunk and looking for trouble, Baley went to the ranch of one Edgar Reed, who was a very peaceable man, and started harassing Mr. Reed. The first thing that Edgar Reed did was to pick up a rusty old horseshoeing rasp (in those days they were eighteen inches long and three eighths of an inch thick) and knocked Baley Hurd clear out of the blacksmith shop. After getting to his feet, Baley came charging back inside. About then, Edgar reached into his saddle bag and pulled out an old 32-20 Colt Revolver and discharged it square into Baley's face. Luck was really riding with Baley that day; he must have had an angel on each shoulder. The bullet nicked the top of his ear just enough to draw blood, and it clipped a lock of hair off as it sped on by his head. Baley stopped dead in his tracks. After a few seconds said, "Why you mangy old farmer, you would have killed me wouldn't you?"

Edgar Reed replied, "You're damned right I would have, and I might do it yet if you don't get on that horse and get the hell out of here." Reed's message was clear. A much more sober Baley Hurd mounted his horse and rode off towards home.

Another of Baley's memorable fights was with a man by the name of Gus (short for Augustus) Wescott who also lived in the community of Cedar. A big man, Wescott was several inches taller and about forty pounds heavier than Baley. He damn sure wasn't accustomed to being whipped by anyone. These two men

101

were the same age and not unlike two young bulls. Because they both had sound reputations for being good fighters, these two probably started an altercation just to see who was the best. For over two hours, the men fought sometimes on the ground but mostly on their feet. When they were finally as bloody as a bull in a bullfight and both were hurt bad, they didn't have the strength to continue. Finally, Gus took one last fall to the ground and was unable to get up. He couldn't see; both eyes were swollen shut. Because both ears were full of blood and so puffed up they were nearly closed, he could barely hear. He still tried to continue the fight by crawling along the ground and reaching out hoping to get a hold of Baley's leg. After a brief try at this, he completely collapsed. Baley and some of the people who had gathered around to watch the show carried Gus into the house and deposited him onto a bed. Delirious, he wouldn't stay put. Subconsciously, he still wanted to be out there fighting, but Baley was through with the competition and chose to sit up all night with Gus. Afraid that no one else would take good enough care of him and that he might die, Baley talked to him, consoled him, gave him water, and occasionally whiskey. Gus's lips were so battered and cut up, he could barely drink. Baley kept cool wet towels on Gus' face and bathed the bruised areas all night. Until he was sure that Gus Wescott was going to be all right, he never once cared for his own wounds, which were plentiful. This was typical of Baley Hurd's personality though. While he might fight a man one minute, Baley would be the first one to come forward if the same man needed a friend or help.

Very shortly after this bruising altercation with Wescott, Baley had an opportunity to help a young cowboy who, by virtue of his curiosity and interest in gold coins and poker, had inadvertently stood too close to a card table (a no-no for the lookers-on who like to watch high-stakes gambling) and thereby angered a sore loser whose pile of gold coins was declining rapidly.

Sam Bankston, a Disappointment Valley cattleman, and his fifteen-year-old son Bud had driven a bunch of cattle to the stockyards at Placerville, Colorado to ship them on the railroad. After seeing the cattle loaded and on their way to market, the father and son found Placerville to be a little too tame for their style of fun. They decided to go on up to Telluride where there was more of everything that goes along with an evening of fun and relaxation. Since there was no evening train out of Placerville, the cowboys secured the services of "Dewey" Greager and his model "T" taxi (See Chapter Five, "A Cowboy in the Family") and arrived shortly in the booming mining town of Telluride, Colorado.

They proceeded to a local saloon and card emporium and, after having a couple of drinks at the bar, decided to watch a little gambling. The young cowboy, Bud Bankston, just happened to be a nephew of Baley Hurd's employer, Joe Bankston. Neither Sam nor Bud knew that Baley was in town that day nor that he would soon come to their rescue.

Bud was entranced by the stacks of bright, gold coins that were moved across the table with each bet that was made. Disappointment Valley had never hosted this form of gambling; this was Bud's first trip to a place like Telluride. A sore-loser at the table thought Bud was standing too close to the action and was certain this was causing his string of bad luck. Without any warning, he got up from his chair and smashed a fist into Bud's face knocking him to the floor. A huge, hard-rock miner with a very hard-case reputation, the gambler jerked Bud up from the floor and smashed him with another blow to the face. Barely fifteen years old, poor Bud had never been handled so violently before and had neither the chance nor the skill to defend himself. With his badly broken nose bleeding profusely and with two teeth already knocked out, he looked a sight. When his attacker prepared to deliver yet a third punch to Bud's face, a huge right hand came out of nowhere and sent the miner reeling.

Before he could regain his balance or determine where this new threat came from, another mallet-sized fist sent him sprawling to the floor. Baley Hurd yanked him erect and delivered another bone-crunching blow to the battered, bleeding countenance of this ugly-customer. The burly, hard-case miner who, moments before, had been the "bully of the town" and "top dog" over a fifteen year-old kid, was now reduced to a helpless, beaten hulk. Taking him under the arms, Baley dragged him out through the swinging doors (no small job even for a man as powerful as Baley Hurd) and dumped him unceremoniously into the street with these words of advice, "If I ever again hear of you beating up on a defenseless, fifteen year-old kid, what I will do to you then will be so bad that this little demonstration won't even be considered a beginning." With that settled, Baley took Bud by the arm and walked him down to a bath house where he could wash him up and assess his wounds.

Baley's own pugnaciousness was bound to be his downfall though. When he was drunk, he just couldn't keep from getting into fights. If he had gotten damn good and whipped sometime, perhaps things might have turned out differently. If he had left John Lavender alone, the shooting incident that cost him his life probably would never have happened.

In the summer, Baley and Mamie moved with the cattle up on North Mountain and lived in a cabin on Bankston Point where the pasture would hold the cattle for the summer. Plenty of lush grass made it an ideal summer place. On a trip back and forth from Cedar to North Mountain one day, Baley spotted a place on Klondike Ridge that he knew would be an excellent place for setting up a still and making whiskey. Water and firewood were in abundance, and best of all, the area was well concealed. Also, he knew his employment with a cattle outfit would be a good cover. With a few friends to keep things going, he knew he could have a pretty good operation. Baley arranged to borrow a still that the owners weren't going to be using for awhile. Once he was set up and had the proper ingredients cooking, Baley was soon bottling his first batch of moonshine whiskey. Because someone had to sample the product to see what the quality of the whiskey was, Baley brought a couple of jugs down to the Joe Bankston place where he and the men who had helped him get started in the moonshine business had a few toasts to the first batch. (The men were Ace Bruce, Clyde Crable, Jim Broiles, Joe Bankston and Baley Hurd.) A little while later, John Lavender came riding down the road. Since there was plenty to go around, they hailed him to join them. He tied his horse in the Chico Brush across a small arroyo, walked over to the cabin, and entered.

Born and raised in Disappointment Valley, John Lavender was a local cowboy who had never gotten into any real trouble—nothing more serious than a half dozen fist fights. Still, some townspeople thought he didn't work very hard at avoiding trouble if it came around. Many people in the Nucla, Colorado area had this impression of John Lavender: "Here's a man who could ride a running horse down a fenced lane, and holding the bridle reins in his teeth, shoot tin cans from the fence posts with a pistol in each hand." How anyone could get a reputation like that without working at it is hard to figure. Incidents like his fight with Golman Garner, where he brazenly rode right into the ranchyard of Mr. Garner and renewed a long standing and bitter dispute over grass and water rights, bolstered people's claim that John deserved the tough reputation of someone to leave alone. If it hadn't been for an old oil-soaked, corroded black powder cartridge that misfired, he never would have survived that day. Upon seeing her husband challenged and witnessing the first exchange of fists being landed, Garner's wife grabbed up a pistol, concealed it in her apron pocket, and rushed out to the defense of her husband. Just as she reached the two men, John Lavender was knocked to the ground but came up with a pitchfork in his hands. At this sudden turn of events, Mrs.

Garner rushed up to John. Without hesitation, she pressed the barrel of her gun into the side of his head and pulled the trigger. A very disappointing click was all that followed, but that didn't alter her original plan of protecting her husband. When the gun didn't fire, she instantly clubbed Lavender over the head with it, and gave him a terrible gash that bled profusely. As quick as he could gather up his hat and wit, John Lavender mounted his horse and rode away. He probably figured he had used up his share of luck for that day.

John Lavender and Clyde Crable were both working cowboys for the cattleman Ed Lavender (no relation to John). They rode together, ate together, and sometimes even had to share the same bedroll. They were together again, in the cabin that day. While drinking with their friends, they suddenly, and, for no apparent reason, erupted into a full scale fist fight. Lavender was clearly getting the best of it; for all practical purposes, Clyde Crable was soon whipped. When John wouldn't stop beating on him, Baley finally stepped between them and said, "He's had enough, John."

To this Lavender replied, "I'll say when he's had enough," and he started trying to get at Crable again. At this point, Baley knocked Lavender to the floor and called him a few choice names. John was slow getting to his feet but when he did he said, "I'll kill you for that, Baley Hurd."

Baley just laughed and said, "You ain't gonna kill anybody, so get the hell out of here." John got on his horse and rode away, but when he reached the gate, he did not turn down the road towards his home; instead he turned back up Disappointment Creek from where he had come. To several of the men in the cabin, there was a foreboding significance to the turn John made in going back up the creek.

After riding two miles to the ranch of a friend, Jack Wescott, Lavender greeted him and said, "I'd like to borrow your gun, Jack."

Said Mr. Wescott, "What do you need with a gun, John?"

Lavender replied, "I want to kill a coyote." Jack said he guessed he could borrow it for that all right. He went into the house and brought out his new Savage .22 Hi-Power rifle. At that time, that rifle was the ultimate in high intensity cartridges; it had become very popular as a varmint and predator caliber because of its extremely flat trajectory and inherent accuracy. John accepted the rifle, thanked Mr. Wescott, and rode back down toward the Bankston Cabin.

At the beginning of that day, John Lavender had never had a thought of trouble with Baley Hurd. Baley had carved his niche among the fighting men when he administered a bad beating to Gus Wescott. After that, he was not bothered by men wanting to pick a fight just for the thrill of it, but John Lavender had just been humiliated in front of men who held considerable respect for him. He had been knocked to the floor, cursed, and then practically kicked out of the company of his friends. Small wonder that all rational thoughts had deserted him. The only thought in his mind now was to get even and humiliate Baley Hurd. Lavender had the means to do it right there in his hands. Knowing that Baley had a deathly fear of guns, John Lavender thought this might be the way to make him crawl and beg for mercy.

Meanwhile, back at the Bankston Cabin, the men had gathered outside by the corrals; some were getting ready to leave. Baley had mentioned that Mamie would be home from the school house pretty quick, and he had better jingle up the milk cow. When they looked up the road, they saw John riding back. Jim Broiles said, "Baley, yonder comes John, and he's got a gun."

Baley replied, "Ah, don't worry, he won't use it." Baley finished putting the saddle on his horse. By then Lavender was in the ranch yard.

Another of the men said to Baley rather urgently, "You'd

better get the hell out of here, Baley. He means to kill you."
Quickly looking over his shoulder, Baley saw Lavender with the
gun pointed squarely at him. He whirled around towards his
horse and was reaching for the saddle horn to mount when a
shot blasted the evening stillness. Baley's right arm dropped
lifeless to his side; his elbow was shattered and spurting blood.
The horse reared away and stampeded down through the pasture
with the fragments of the bullet imbedded in his jaw. John
Lavender mounted his horse and rode away. When Clyde Crable
came out of the cabin to see what was going on, he saw Baley
down on the ground holding his arm. Seeing so much blood all
around, he rushed back into the cabin and grabbed up some
washed-out flour sacks and went out to help Baley. Unable to
stop the flow of blood, he put a tourniquet above the wound and
went for help. After Clyde found Mamie at the school house,
they managed to find someone with a car to take Baley into
Norwood. Charley Mair lived the closest and he had a car, so it's
a good bet that he was the one who took Baley to Norwood to
find a doctor. All the way out to Norwood from Cedar, Baley
said repeatedly that he didn't want John Lavender prosecuted
over the shooting incident. He said after he got well he would
take care of Lavender in his own way. After quite a bit of
looking around, they finally found Dr. Bollinger delivering a
baby in the community of Redvale. As fate would have it, the
woman in labor was none other than the one, who, as a little girl
many years before, had lost her magnificent butterfly costume
in the chaos created by Baley Hurd's display of anger. Now,
Baley clung to life in the front yard of the woman who had
(unbeknownst to him) held a grudge against him for these many
years because of the loss of her prize costume. Dr. Bollinger
was called outside to have a look at Baley. Discouraged at the
condition of Baley's arm, he told him that he was not equipped
to do anything for it. The tourniquet had not been loosened since
it was put on, and the blood vessels were surely very badly

damaged. After Dr. Bollinger loosened the tourniquet for a short while and then re-tightened it, he sent them to see Dr. Tidd in Telluride, where there were hospital facilities. He then returned to the house and the laboring woman. In Telluride, Baley Hurd was admitted immediately. After two days of a steadily deteriorating condition, Dr. Tidd told Baley that gangrene had set in where the blood vessels were badly damaged. Because he could not stop the spread of it, he would have to amputate the arm at the shoulder. Feeling bad for him, Mamie cried at the thought of him losing his arm. "Don't you worry about it, Mamie, I'll learn to use my left hand and be just as good with it as I was with the right." Baley also impressed upon Dr. Tidd that he didn't want anybody messing around prosecuting John Lavender. He still wanted that job for himself. Sadly, it turned out to be a deathbed statement.

Dr. Tidd proceeded with the operation to amputate Baley's arm, but the old fighter never regained consciousness. Had he been treated in the very beginning for shock and loss of blood and had his wound been bound up with a pressure bandage, he probably would have survived the ordeal with his arm intact. As it was, he went into anesthetic shock during the operation and later died. The doctors of that day knew little of the complications which ultimately killed Baley Hurd.

The date of his passing was January 26, 1921. He was buried in the Placerville Cemetery beside his two babies and his younger brother who had met a very untimely death in 1918. I expect that Baley Hurd's funeral was the largest ever held in Placerville.

After the funeral, Mamie went back to Cedar to dispose of their property and to terminate her job at the school. When Ern Maupin heard that Mamie was selling everything, he made a fast trip to Cedar. Because of his fondness for Baley and wanting something to remember him by, he purchased the big sorrel horse that still had the fragments of bullet imbedded in his jaw.

Of the hundreds of horses that Baley had handled for Ern Maupin, this one would be the last horse Ern would ever own that had been broken and trained by the skillful and dedicated horseman, Baley Hurd.

The baby who was being born as Baley Hurd lay dying grew up to learn of her fleeting connection with the untimely death of this illustrious man. For years she prodded her parents to tell her about Baley Hurd. After years of being rebuffed by her mother, who was annoyed at the child's curiousity about this man, the little girl finally hit a nerve when, one day, she suddenly asked her mother if she had been *afraid* of Baley Hurd. In exasperation, her mother replied that she had not been afraid of Baley Hurd. Her only thoughts of the man had been those of her anger towards him for breaking up the Halloween Dance and causing the destruction of the butterfly wings her mother had made for her. The little girl's connection to Baley Hurd finally became clear to her; she decided that she was being born at the exact same time that Baley Hurd most needed a doctor's attention because, in the child's own words many years later, "A malicious fate of long memory was playing a macabre joke on Baley Hurd in order to even the score for the destruction of Mama's butterfly wings." Interesting place, the mind of a child!

Chapter 11

A WINTER CAMP IN INDIAN VALLEY

Indian Valley. A beautiful name for a beautiful place located in the lower Disappointment Valley near the old community of Cedar. It is situated up in the pinon and juniper benches rising toward Glade Mountain.

In 1882 the area was known mostly by the Ute Indians. They loved it as a hunting ground and must have used it for centuries. There is no place in southwestern Colorado that has produced as many arrowheads and artifacts per square yard, as Indian Valley. Also, there is evidence that they must have spent time preparing their food here because *manos* and *metates* have been discovered all over the area. (*Manos* and *metates* are special stones that are used together to grind corn, seeds, nuts, et cetera.)

In the early winter of 1882, a man named Matt Hammond found this beautiful place in the company of four of his fellow packers. They had left the Rico area when winter snows forced them to take their horses and pack animals to seek a milder climate in which to spend the winter. They traveled for days down the Dolores River drainage. As they were being pushed on by cattlemen and ranchers moving their stock, the men forded the Dolores and crossed over Glade Mountain. After finding Indian Valley, they knew this was a place where they could spend the winter; there was ample forage for the horses and mules and a sheltered, sunny valley to set up a camp. On a large sandstone rock near the mouth of the valley, the men inscribed their names or initials. The inscription of the date, December 25, 1882, is still quite clear today. Time and weather have wreaked havoc on all but the inscriptions of the names of Matt Hammond, Bullock, and Howard Richardson. These names are also still quite legible today.

Down country about a mile or two to the northwest, into Lower Disappointment, another camp of people was well established. It was the family of R. B. Dunham and his wife and her brother, Bill Dawson, who had come to the area from Missouri. Dawson Draw in the area is named for Bill Dawson, who settled in that spot one year later.

That first winter was very hard on both camps. Because the deer had completely left the area, the Dunhams found themselves digging in the snow for the deer bones that they had thrown away earlier in the winter; they re-cooked the bones for the bits of meat and fat to make soup. The Dunham party were determined to stay on and establish homesteads.

In the camp of Matt Hammond, who were all there only for the winter, about the only food they had to eat were biscuits and coffee. The man named Howard Richardson, however, did have in his possession a gallon jug of molasses that he had purchased as a gift for his sweetheart in Dolores. (Her name was Ruby Wallace and he planned to present the gift to her when he went through the area the coming spring.) The camp of hungry men tried just about every way imaginable to get Richardson to share the molasses with them (except forcefully taking it away). Although a little of that sweet stuff sure would make those dry biscuits go down a little easier, the molasses remained unopened and intact until spring. The group did survive the winter after a fashion. When spring did finally arrive, they gathered their horses and what was left of the pack string (several animals had perished during the brutal winter), loaded the camp, and set out for Dolores and Rico.

112

When the men reached the crossing at Beaver Creek, they found it to be in full flood and too dangerous to cross. After spending the night there, they prepared to cross early the next morning when the flood crest was at its lowest. Taking every precaution with his precious jug of molasses, Richardson rolled it up in his bedroll and lashed it securely to a pack animal. Proceeding with the dangerous crossing, they all made it safely to the other side except the pack horse carrying the molasses. The horse lost his footing in the swift undertow, fell, and was washed away. With dismay and frustration, the group watched as the animal rolled over and over down the flooding creek with no hope of being saved. The irony of the molasses jug being washed away as well hit Richardson hard, and he was just grateful that none of the men in the group had suffered or perished during the winter because of his shortsightedness.

About the same time that Matt Hammond was leaving the camp in Indian Valley, his brother, Allan Hammond, and a man named Joe Davis (for whom Joe Davis Canyon is named) brought the first herd of cattle into Disappointment. These two men and yet another Joe Davis (no relation) went to Utah and bought a herd from a man by the name of Al Scorup. They had planned to bring the cattle back through Monticello and into Dissapointment from the Dove Creek Area. This was the year after the Utes had been removed to the Reservation, and the resentful Indians had gone on the warpath in the Moab-Blanding area. When Hammond heard of this development, he felt it necessary to change plans. The men decided to trail their herd around by Red Lake, Arizona. From there, they would take them in behind the Sleeping Ute mountain near Cortez. At this point they crossed Montezuma Valley, the Dolores River, over Glade Mountain, and finally into Disappointment Valley.

Once settled with the cattle in Disappointment, the branding began. The brand used was "AN," presumably for Allen and his son Norman. The "AN" cattle were kept for many years and were recognized as being the first cattle herd in Disappointment Valley.

At the mouth of an area called Pine Arroyo, Allan homesteaded a place. With the help of another man, he began digging a well. They had the well pretty far along, and, one day, after breaking for lunch, Hammond was lowered down into the well to resume digging. While waiting for the bucket to be lowered, he lit his pipe. As the match was lit, there was a great whoosh; his hat and pipe both came flying up out of the well. Hammond wasn't harmed any, but he was certainly mystified by the explosion. Ironically, to date, gas exploration in the area has been anything but encouraging.

An excellent blacksmith, Allan Hammond made all the tools needed on his ranch. One of his finest accomplishments was a pair of dental forceps that he made after several sleepless nights with an unbearable toothache. He handed the forceps to one of the ranch hands and said, "Here, pull this tooth." The man obliged, but he pulled the wrong tooth. Hammond told him to put the tooth back in the socket, showed him the tooth that was hurting, and instructed him to get it right this time. The tooth that was mistakenly pulled, rooted back. It is said that it was one of the last to be pulled when Hammond got his false teeth many years later.

Another emergency measure for toothaches in early Disappointment was related by Mable Stoddard who was married to a man named Vossburg. Having reached the end of his ability to tolerate a miserable toothache, he decided to put a grain of lye in the cavity. When asked later, "Didn't that hurt," he is said to have replied, "Boy I'll say, but it sure did feel good when it quit."

Some people may wonder why such a beautiful and productive valley got the name Disappointment. The explanation that I have always been the fondest of is this:

When the first group of settlers came into the lower end of

the valley, by way of Slickrock, they had been traveling for days through dry, desolate, barren and rocky country. Looking up the valley they could make out a long line of green Cottonwood trees. Because this surely meant a stream of clear, running water, they eagerly pressed on. Upon reaching the banks where they expected to see a stream, they instead saw stagnant, alkali pools, too strong even for thirsty livestock. Recalling the feelings of the group later, said the leader of the party it was "utter disappointment."

Chapter 12

THE HISTORY OF THE GURLEY RESERVOIR

One Hundred Years

October 1, 1989 will mark the one hundred year anniversary of water storage at the site known today as the Gurley Reservoir. The history of this important storage facility provides an education in the early land and water deals that spawned the vast network of irrigation canals and water storage facilities so vital to the agricultural growth of San Miguel and Montrose Counties.

"There's an empire to be had out there and it's ours for the taking. All we have to do is go out and get it. What do you say, Walt?" The land being referred to by Charles Gurley was the western slope of Colorado. In 1881, the recently published Hayden Survey gave glowing accounts of the vast grazing lands. The high mountains contained rushing streams just waiting to be re-routed into great canals and transported to the semi-arid land that lay in uncounted thousands of acres. Still

The three circle brand of the Naturita Cattle and Land Company. (Courtesy of the Museum of Western Colorado, the Wilson Rockwell Collection.)

unsurveyed, this land was unclaimed except by the Uncompaghre Ute Indians. The Brunot Treaty of 1874 was supposed to have removed the Indians from most of Western Colorado. Their new home was to be the Uncompaghre Valley; after a few years, they would lose that too. When that land was opened for settling in 1881, the Utes were moved to reservations farther south.

Walter Wheeler's reply to Gurley was, "Let's go for it. I can get the cattle and I know that a lot of Colorado ranch corporations are returning profits of forty percent or better." This speculative conversation took place in Denver, Colorado sometime during the year 1881.

The Homestead Act gave people the right to claim land that was available in 160 acre tracts. However, out in the semi-arid West where land was plentiful, the Government set the size of the homestead much larger; 640 acres in some cases and, where irrigation was possible (on twenty acres at least), the tract size was 320 acres. Called desert claims, they could be had for $1.25 an acre. The tract size permitting up to 320 acres didn't go into effect until 1894 when the Carey Act was legislated. This law was passed to correct the weaknesses of the Desert Land Act of 1877; this was the first Congressional Act to require irrigation as a condition for privatizing the land. The Government described desert land as "all lands exclusive of timber lands and mineral lands which will not, without irrigation, produce an agricultural crop."

Under the Desert Land Act, a large number of frauds were committed. Land was claimed but no attempts were made to irrigate it. Rather than the actual settlers, cattle companies were obtaining land which they would then sell to settlers and make large profits. Congress intended the act to operate strictly in favor of those who would reclaim lands from desert conditions and render them productive; the purpose was not to permit entries by those who were mere dummies for others who would acquire, hold, and dispose of these homestead entries for speculative purposes.

With the help of Frank Johnson, George S. Burrows and Edward F. Bishop, Walter F. Wheeler and Charles D. Gurley, started laying the plans for a land and cattle empire. Western San Miguel and western Montrose Counties were the areas they chose for the operation. Walt Wheeler would buy the needed cattle in Texas and trail them to the unlimited ranges of the chosen area. A trail already existed because Moses W. Powell had brought a herd of Texas cattle into this same area in 1880. Also, James Galloway, who settled with his family in Paradox, brought a herd by this same route in 1881. By the time Wheeler arrived with his herd in 1882, Charles Gurley and the rest of the group had already laid all the groundwork for the corporation. On February 6, 1884, they incorporated at $500,000 and called their corporation The Naturita Cattle and Land Company. By March 17, 1884, all the members of the corporation had certificates of paid up stock.

After homesteads were obtained for each of them (one for their wives and one for each of their children), there remained one more way to obtain land; a practice that became almost a condition of employment. Employees would obtain a piece of land for a homestead. Then, if they wanted to keep their job, they were expected to sell out to the corporation that fed and clothed them. Most did, and this scheme put the wheels in motion for the next move, which would be to enhance the land values. This was done by spawning an irrigation company under the name of Naturita Canal and Reservoir Company. To Finance it, The Naturita Cattle and Land Company pledged $38,000 for reservoirs and ditches. The owners pledged all of the company's assets to issue $140,000 of joint corporate gold bonds, due and payable in 1906 at six and one half percent interest to The State Trust Company Of New York City. The pledged assets of The Naturita Cattle and Land Company were as follows: 1800 head of cattle and the range they claimed between the San Miguel and Dolores Rivers, two to five miles wide and sixty miles long, from various places on the northwest base of the Lone Cone Mountain to where the Dolores River crosses the Paradox Valley at Bedrock. In the little community of Bedrock, Colorado, The Naturita Cattle and Land Company had purchased a ranch and all of the personal belongings of Theophilus Neathery, who was a brother of "Uncle Dick" Neathery, whose claim to fame was a thoroughbred racehorse known as Sagebrush Jack. This horse was matched twice against a Disappointment Valley cowpony, owned by the Nash outfit, who went by the rather unglamorous name of Swayback Johnny. One win and one loss—and everyone wound up about even. The Naturita Cattle and Land Company also got the Three Circle brand that became so well known on their stock for the next twenty years.

The next step up the ladder of success was to obtain the necessary water. Fifty cubic feet per second (cfs.) was appropriated from the waters of West Beaver Creek and Little Beaver Creek (later to be called Goat Creek after a group of irate Norwood cattlemen stampeded a herd of trespassing goats belonging to a Sanborn Park rancher over about a 200 foot-high cliff and killed them all). Reservoir Site One would be in Section thirty-six, Township forty-four north, Range Line twelve and west of the New Mexico Principal Meridian. This first storage facility, The Naturita Canal and Reservoir Company Reservoir one, was built in 1889 after the Governor of Colorado agreed to deed the entire section to the The Naturita Canal and Reservoir Company on April 22nd of that year. He had extracted the promise that the reservoir would be constructed and an operating canal system ready for use on or before October 1, 1889. The first storage was 199 acre-feet with an acre-foot of water consisting of 325,000 gallons.

Naturita Cattle and Land Company started advertising for

people to move into the area and settle the land. There was land and water aplenty for any and all comers—forty acres of land and forty shares of water for a price. In this particular system, one share was an amount of water calculated to irrigate one acre over the growing season. Due to some creative interpretation of

The author's father (without moustache) with three of his very good friends (*left to right*: Roger Williams, Max Malich, and Jacob Fisk) at a Denver stock show in 1914. All but Mr. Greager had moved to the area to buy land and water from Naturita Cattle & Land Co.

the Desert Land Act of 1877, The Naturita Cattle and Land Company already owned most of the land. After acquiring the land, the company made no attempt to irrigate it until its system was in operation. Feeling justified in securing land by any means possible, the cattlemen had to protect certain water rights for their cattle and also needed a migration route open from winter range to summer range. Their very existence depended on having control of these things. Then the land, with its ready supply of water, was turned over for sale. Until the Carey Act of 1894 was in effect, they would have ten years of unlimited expansion. Up until 1894, all that was needed to verify a claim to a homestead entry was to have two credible witnesses to swear about the boundaries or improvements. Since it was all unsurveyed at the time, boundaries were described in a manner such as: "Beginning at that big rock on the ridge, south to that old snag pine and then east across the flat, to the point of the ridge where that draw begins; going north down the draw to the rim of the canyon and then along the rim of the canyon back to the first mentioned big rock; containing 160 acres, more or less." The big outfits probably had an ample supply of credible witnesses. In their eagerness to get areas like this settled, the government would set up a land office in close proximity to the land. That's why a land office was established in the little town of Redvale, Colorado. E. L. McKee was the first land agent, and land entries could be made in less than a day.

Buyers for the land were plentiful and arrived well ahead of the water. Promises on top of promises that the water would be there any day failed to hold some of them. Many of the people who had bought land sight unseen sold it back to the land company at a loss after waiting as much as two years for the water. The irrigation system reached partial completion by 1887, for three years, both The Naturita Canal and Reservoir Company and The Naturita Cattle and Land Company enjoyed tremendous growth. However, along with the dreams of the founders being realized, is was also becoming painfully clear that they had not filed on enough water.

The Shenandoah Irrigation and Land Company was formed on February 7, 1887 to buy out The Naturita Canal and Reservoir Company. The Board of Directors included: William D. Morrison, a Denver financier, Jess Barnes, local land owner and entrepreneur, and Charles D. Gurley, who was on the board of directors of both The Naturita Cattle and Land Company and The Naturita Canal and Reservoir Company. The Shenandoah Irrigation and Land Company incorporated and issued five hundred $1000 Corporate Gold Bonds through The International Trust Company of New York City. The Naturita Canal and Reservoir Company was paid $30,000 in cash, and a payment was to be made twice a year until all of the gold bonds were redeemed. The Shenandoah group changed the name to The Naturita Ditch Company and operated the system until 1906.

The Shenandoah group had plans to send water to the West Lilylands via a canal that would cross Broad Canyon around the mouth of Hamilton Canyon and then grade out towards West Lilylands. They had envisioned a 20,000 acre development that would become the sugar beet capitol of the world with a processing plant and the works. The Norwood-Redvale-Shenandoah development would eventually consist of about 32,000 acres. However, the plans for the canals that would flow wide and clear didn't materialize. They were hard pressed to maintain the company as it was. Roderick A. Gurley, brother of Charles D. Gurley became vice-president of the company in 1891. At this time the debts of the company still exceeded $11,000 over and above the corporate gold bonds.

More water was the prime concern now. On March 12, 1897, the second decree for 12.5 cfs. was filed on. This decree came out of Middle Beaver, East Beaver and various branches of East Beaver. This required the construction of the Beaver Extension as the present storage intake system began at West Beaver. The contract for the construction was awarded to J. E. Sandy and S. A. Kemp, who moved a big steam powered shovel to the site and completed the canal in record time. While they were in the area, an enlargement was done on the existing West Beaver system so it could handle the additional flow of water.

About this time, The Naturita Canal and Reservoir Company sold Reservoir Site One to The Naturita Ditch Company. With the irrigation company having filed on more water and with the purchase of the reservoir site, everything seemed to be pointing to a successful takeover by the Shenandoah group.

While The Naturita Canal and Reservoir Company only sold water and land as a package, The Naturita Ditch Company would sell water to anybody who wanted it and had the money to pay for it. Two people in the Shenandoah area who bought land and later bought water were John Larson and Anton Skalla. The cost of the water entailed a $200 down payment and $588 a year for nine years; that was for 1/2 cfs., if and when it was available. The land that Skalla owned was purchased from the Homestead of Harrietta Gurley, wife of Charles D. Gurley.

The Naturita Ditch Company could only serve about half of Wright's Mesa. This left about 10,000 acres of prime land that could not be irrigated under the present ditch system; practically all of it was taken up by settlers. In 1902, the settlers who were not being served with water, banded together and started building an irrigation system for themselves. They named their group The Lone Cone Ditch and Reservoir Company, and its survey called for bringing the water down the west side of Wright's Mesa. The company filed on water from Naturita Creek at its headwaters. In a few years they had canals built and a small storage facility (851 acre feet) completed. The farmers labored on the canals and Reservoir to pay for their stock (or shares) in the company. Although they had operated for several years without the benefit of storage, having this second source of irrigation water considerably aided the settling and developing of the Norwood-Redvale-Shenandoah area. The site of the storage facility they built was actually on the property of The Naturita Ditch Company, which was called Reservoir Site Two. In 1911, The Lone Cone Ditch and Reservoir Company was able to purchase this reservoir site and after a resurvey was made by A. M. Browning, expansion work commenced on the site which today is known as the Cone Reservoir. The construction was done by Skidmore Brothers beginning on August 25, 1911, and was accepted for filing with the County Clerk on February 4, 1913. The final capacity was 4225 acre feet.

Even though The Naturita Canal and Reservoir Company was not actively distributing water then, it was still a bonafide corporation. On May 2, 1893, the corporation purchased water rights out of Beaver Creek from a placer mining company known as The San Miguel Hydraulic Mining Company. The company had come into possession of it through a quitclaim deed from The Keokuk Hydraulic Mining Company, which in turn had purchased it through an assignment of rights from one Lewis Green. Having appropriated the water from Beaver Creek he transported it via a ditch a little over five miles long to a stream that was known as Saltado Creek. The water was then conveyed down the stream bed approximately four miles. Here, a headgate discharged the water into yet another ditch which in turn carried the water to a reservoir on a point overlooking the San Miguel River. This point has since been known as Reservoir Point. The water from this reservoir was piped down the mountainside to the site of the placers and furnished the water pressure for hydraulic mining. The remains of these workings are plainly seen across the San Miguel River about halfway between the mouth of Saltado Creek and the mouth of Specie Creek. Lewis Green was paid $5,000 for the water rights on the 12th of March, 1881. He had come into that area in 1877 with a surveying party who were locating placer claims for a large mining concern. After they located about nine placer claims, Green immediately started work on the ditches. He had appropriated 4,000 miner inches of water (approx. 104 cfs.), but his ditches were never big enough to handle that much flow. Four or five cfs. would have been sufficient to maintain the reservoir at a very high level. The construction of the ditch had to be done with teams and plows and scrapers and a lot of hard work with picks and shovels.

As the work on this ditch probably started in 1878, I have wondered many times if the work parties didn't have some trouble with the Ute Indians. Many of them had never reported to the Reservation and were roaming around the country, hunting, and camping as they were accustomed to doing. In 1879, one of these small hunting parties happened upon Fred Mayall and his cowboys down near the Coke Ovens*, beat them up and made them eat grass like cattle before stampeding the cowboys' herd and setting the men free. (See Chapter twenty, "The Wild Cattle of the Club Range.") There was also an uprising by the Utes over near Monticello, Utah in 1881. Since this ditch work was done between 1878 and 1881, it seems likely that a band of Indians surely passed through that area and observed what was going on.

A water decree is like money in the bank; it is very valuable. To obtain one, the water must first be appropriated and must have a planned transportation and distribution survey to follow. Then the water has to be put to beneficial use, such as irrigating farmland or filling a reservoir. If the water has not previously been claimed for the same purpose, it can then be decreed to a certain ditch or storage facility or a piece of land. For twelve years, the water rights that Lewis Green sold to The Keokuk Hydraulic Mining Company—had been used beneficially by the two respective mining companies to wash gold from the hillsides that had, a million years ago, been a riverbed. The Naturita Canal and Reservoir Company then owned it for four more years. The rights covered twice as much water as the company presently owned; and the appropriation date made it three years before their first decree of 50 cfs. It should have

---

* The Coke Ovens is a place on Dry Creek, a few miles south of its confluence with the San Miguel River. Here, coal mined in the area was converted into coke, and shipped to the steel mills.

been considered a valuable acquisition; it should have been made a part of the available water for the canal system. The purchase price was $7,500 which, in 1893, was a considerable amount of money. Also, The Naturita Ditch Company was at the zenith of land and water sales at this time. Inconceivably though, these water rights slipped away through negligence or apathy.

The first Water Congress ever held in Colorado was in June of 1897 for the purpose of adjudicting water rights that had been put to beneficial use and to hold conditional those that lacked completion of their projects. The water right appropriated by Lewis Green in 1881 was not decreed by this Congress; no record has ever been found that it was even submitted. The Beaver Extension was completed that summer (1897). Providing the water rights were decreed, it would have been so simple, to just move the point of diversion downstream and pick it up in the new Beaver Extension. Moving a point of diversion downstream is relatively simple compared to trying to go upstream with one. Both of the Naturita Canal's water rights (50 cfs. and 12.5 cfs.) were decreed absolute, as well as was the storage facility, Reservoir Site One, for 199 acre-feet. Perhaps the shrewd minds at the reins of the corporation had other plans for the water rights purchased from the mining company. In the meantime, $7,500 and immeasurably valuable water, went down the drain, never to return.

In 1906, The Naturita Ditch Company defaulted on its payments to The Naturita Canal and Reservoir Company, and a federal court in Denver ordered a reconveyance of title back to the parent company. Shortly after this exchange took place, The Naturita Canal and Reservoir Company filed on an additional 17.5 cfs., which was its third decree out of Beaver Creek. This necessitated more enlargement of the canal system. A couple of years prior to this, W. H. Nelson had formed a small irrigation company and tapped the flow of Dempsey Creek, Spring Creek,

McCullough Creek, and some of East Beaver. His own ditch system (Nelson Ditch) proved difficult to maintain, so he made his intake system flow into the Beaver Extension and enlarged the canal to enable it to carry up to 105 cfs. more water. Not wanting his water to go into storage, he routed it around the reservoir and back into the Naturita Canal. A headgate discharged his water into another section of the Nelson Ditch and carried the water to its destination—800 acres of farmland northeast of the town of Norwood. The Nelson Ditch was constructed for several more miles towards Mailbox Park but was not used until it was purchased by The San Miguel Development Company.

On May 29, 1907, The Naturita Canal and Reservoir Company entered into an agreement with A. E. Guy to enlarge its entire system. From a flow that was guaranteed to be 60 cfs. Mr. Guy agreed to boost the amount of water to 200 cfs. Planning to develop Mailbox Park, he wished to run a canal over there. Terms of the agreement stated that A. E. Guy would furnish the teams, plows, scrapers, and all of the labor to do the work. He would be refinanced by a commission of twenty-five dollars a share on all the stock he could sell on The Naturita Canal and Reservoir Company. A. E. Guy was a banker who operated a bank in Norwood, Colorado.

On September 9, 1907, The Naturita Canal and Reservoir Company went into receivership. The lifetime of the corporation had expired, and apparently the board of directors did not choose to renew the certificate. Walter F. Wheeler, for one, was heavily involved in mining and was a principal owner of the famous "Lizzie G" gold and silver mine near the town of Sawpit, Colorado. For years, Charles D. Gurley had been involved with locating and selling placer claims. Two of the most notable of these claims were the "Kentucky" and the "Rock Gap," which were bought by Moses D. Powell, the earliest big cattleman on Wright's Mesa. The time had come, and something had to be done with the irrigation company. After Frank Gove was appointed as the trustee, litigation was initiated to dispose of the corporation. In 1908, The Empire Irrigation and Land Company was formed by mortgaging The Naturita Canal and Reservoir Company and The Naturita Cattle and Land Company to The State Trust Company of New York City. Shortly before this new irrigation company had taken control, a Norwood rancher and businessman, Henry Copp, filed a lawsuit on November 12, 1907 to stop The Naturita Canal and Reservoir Company from selling stock certificates and entitling the purchasers thereof to prorate with Copp and other water-users in the 50 cfs. Priority One out of West Beaver. This was the beginning of the second and third decree conflict that took several years to settle. The third decree for 17.5 cfs. which had been filed on March 12, 1907, was expected to help ease the situation that brought about the court action. During the preceding year the capacity of the main Naturita Canal and Reservoir Site One had been enlarged to 702 acre-feet. The construction was completed on May 30, 1906, and The Empire Irrigation and Land Company operated the system for several years. There doesn't seem to be any exact date when the reservoir became known as Gurley; I don't believe there were any dedication ceremonies. The last elected officers of The Naturita Canal and Reservoir Company were Roderick A. Gurley, president, and Charles D. Gurley, vice-president and Jess Barnes, secretary. When that ditch company went into receivership (because of some formal business code) and the Reservoir was sold separately to The Empire Irrigation and Land Company in 1908, Roderick and Charles Gurley's signatures were the only ones on the document. Thereafter, the only references made to that transaction were "the deal we made with Gurley." Very soon after that, the reservoir and ditch systems were known as Gurley Reservoir and Gurley Ditch. In 1911, the irrigation company again changed hands. The new owners were The San Miguel

Irrigation and Land Company, which went through the same takeover procedure as its predecessors. The Guardian Savings and Trust Company of Cleveland, Ohio loaned one million dollars to clear the mortgage of The Empire Irrigation Company. During the years of ownership by Empire, the threat of the lawsuit brought by Henry Copp, was hanging over the company's head. Now that the owners had sold out, it was someone else's turn. By the time The San Miguel Irrigation and Land Company had gained control, quite a number of other water-users of the first decree had intervened in the suit. According to the attorneys for the water-users, their action would make a stronger case and force settlement of some kind. In 1913, things started coming to a head. Through a pooling of shares and a redistribution of water on a predetermined plan, a new company called The Farmers Water Development Company emerged from the chaos. A one million dollar loan paid off the indebtedness of The San Miguel Irrigation and Land Company. The second and third decree conflicts were peacefully settled when it was successfully proven that the first decree, which called for 50 cfs. was actually delivering closer to 30 cfs. This loss of approximately 20 cfs. was caused by seepage and evaporation due to transporting the water over long distances by the canal. Therefore, all but 10 cfs. of the second and third decrees (which totaled 30 cfs.) were needed to fulfill the 50 cfs. obligation of the first decree. Sold after the remaining 10 cfs. (from the second and third decrees) were parceled out, the certificates were sound and good. It was also successfully proven that the canals of the distribution system in existence at that time did not have the carrying capacity for the additional water it would take to make the rest of the second and third decree water certificates valid for deliverance of their prescribed amounts.

The Naturita Canal and Reservoir Company had sold water certificates for at least 200 cfs., but at this point in time, it was only delivering 60 cfs. After the water certificates were sold in numerical order, those that were left over (once the 60 cfs. had been allotted) were rendered null and void. In the reorganizational plans for Farmers Water Development Company extra water was filed on, these leftover water certificates were made good for their prescribed amounts. The new company immediately filed on 215 cfs. more water, and the intake canal system was enlarged to handle 300 cfs. About this time, A. M. Browning was hired to conduct an engineering study for raising the dam at Reservoir Site One, or "Gurley," as it was then commonly called, to increase its storage capacity by 2,297.83 acre-feet. The cost of this project was around $26,000; when completed it brought the storage capacity to 3,000 acre-feet. From here on out, the story of The Farmers Water Development Company is one of continuous progress. On November 11, 1936, construction was begun to enlarge the capacity of the reservoir to 9,000 acre-feet. This was completed in 1948. Another major milestone occurred on February 19, 1939 when the inlet canal was decreed to 600 cfs. In 1961, work began to raise the dam to sixty feet high which, when completed, would increase the storage capacity to 10,039 acre feet. The storage decree made possible by this enlargement was made absolute on September 5, 1965.

There have been a few bad years when the snowfall was light and the runoff short; the drought year of 1977 was a good example of how important the snowpack is to the irrigation company. Recent problems with leakage around the dam caused quite a bit of concern among area residents and particularly the water users. In the spring of 1987, the drilling and grouting gave surprisingly good results. The round of drilling and grouting done on the fall of 1988 may have left the dam in good enough condition to warrant full use again. Many dams about the same age as The Gurley Dam have started leaking, as well as some newer ones. Built in 1962, the dam at Miramonte Reservoir began leaking as soon as the lake filled up. Drilling and grouting stopped the majority of the leaks there; nothing more has been required.

The name Gurley is so appropriate. Even though he was here for business reasons only, Charles D. Gurley was one of the very early people on Wright's Mesa. Associated with land and water dealings all over the areas around Norwood and Naturita, he also owned a number of lots in the town of Norwood. However, the Gourley addition to the town of Norwood was named after the man who owned the annexed property, Abraham L. Gourley (note the spelling). Mr. A. L. Gourley also owned some land across Maverick Draw and was the first superintendent of the Norwood Sunday School class.

There is a great potential for more storage reservoirs in San Miguel county. Tentative plans at this date (1989) consider the possibility of rebuilding the Lilylands Reservoir and possibly enlarging the Lone Cone Reservoir. A reservoir site in Dempsey Meadows near Beaver Park has long been on the list of high priority construction, and there has also been talk of a storage facility in Maverick Draw north of Norwood.

Chapter 13

THE FRATERNITY OF WOLVES

Wolves were always a problem in Disappointment Valley. The early Indians told of fearsome raids on their pony herds by packs of wolves in the area. In 1879, a family that had settled there wrote in a letter to relatives in Missouri and told about how they were managing in wintertime and how the wolves had killed nearly all of their chickens.

Allan Hammond mentioned that wolves followed so close behind his sleigh one winter, when they were going home from visiting a neighboring ranch, that he and his wife didn't allow the children to ride in the back-end for fear the wolves would drag them out and kill them. At that time, it was not uncommon for the wolves to come into the barnyard in full daylight, kill young calves, and drag them away. Out on the open range, the stockmen suffered great losses to the roving packs of wolves.

Around 1915, a man they called "Wolf" Morgan came to the valley and started trapping and poisoning wolves for the bounty the stockmen had placed on them. The bounty was around twenty-five dollars per animal whether it was a full-grown wolf or a whelp. By hunting out the dens and destroying the litters, this experienced wolf trapper quickly thinned out their numbers.

A typical trapper of the day, Morgan was a loner; not too well-acquainted with a bathtub, he rarely changed his clothes.

Dirty, bearded, and unkempt, he lived mostly to kill wolves. He was disagreeable and always ready for a fight. When he fought, he behaved like a wolf. "No quarter asked and no quarter given!" he would say. "Win any way you can."

He got into a fight down at Cedar one time with Miles Wescott and cut him up pretty bad with a trapper's knife. Although he would have killed his opponent, Wescott got hold of a double-barreled shotgun. With what strength he had left after the gruesome fight, Wescott busted it over "Wolf" Morgan's head and damn near killed him with one blow. Both men had to be taken to the hospital in Dolores.

Around this same period of time, another "wolfer" by the name of Roy Musselman from Moab, Utah made quite a name for himself by tracking down and destroying the famous cattle-killing wolf known on the Slickhorn Range as "Big Foot." Before Musselman got that job done, he was living exactly like the wolf he was after. Living off the land, eating nuts and berries and an occasional small animal, he slept in very short naps like a wolf and went to the potholes in the rocks for water.

Because they were being killed off in such numbers in Disappointment Valley, the wolves were driven to seek safety in other areas. Until "Wolf" Morgan was set loose, the two neighboring valleys to the northeast of Disappointment, Gypsum and Dry Creek Basin, had never had much of a problem with wolves. An occasional wolf had been seen in remote areas, but the wolf population was not out of control. As a matter of fact, an old cowboy named Edgar Williams knew of an old female wolf that denned up every spring up under Lavender Point. Each spring, he would dig out her whelps (numbering from seven to ten and worth twenty-five dollars apiece). Enjoying this easy way to make a good amount of money, he helped keep the wolf population down for many years. When this old female was killed by a trapper one year, Williams swore an oath of vengeance against all trappers for ruining this easy source of income.

The wolves' migration into these neighboring valleys quickly became a problem for the local stockmen and for yet another well-known trapper of the area. He wasn't concerned with wolves until they invaded the area where he was trapping for smaller animals. His name was Golman Garner, and he had homesteaded in the mouth of Bear Creek in upper Disappointment. If they weren't busy feeding a bunch of cattle, many people in the area became trappers in the wintertime. Since it was one way to escape the boredom of the remote winters and was fairly profitable, it served two purposes at least.

The countryside abounded in bobcats and coyotes, and beaver were plentiful too. The animals Garner mainly trapped were cats. He established a trapline across the top of North Mountain and extended it down into Dry Creek Basin. It took a long, full day to cover the route in one direction. Since he had to spend the night, he had set up for himself a sort of makeshift camp in the head of Broad Canyon. It was just a rock and dirt affair with a pole roof, but it was sufficient for one night's shelter. After spending the night, Garner would head back up Pony Draw and into Horse Park, then to the head of Knight Canyon and down the old mail trail into Disappointment. Most of the trip was made on horseback; in a rare winter, the whole trip could be made that way. When the snow got too deep out on top of North Mountain, Garner would switch to traveling on snowshoes.

One day out in Dry Creek Basin, Garner met up with some cowboys who told him about a pack of wolves that had been killing cattle in the Basin and Gypsum Valleys. The men were concerned about the aggressiveness of the animals and their apparent lack of fear of man. Promising to keep a sharp lookout for them, Garner was kind of anxious to try out a new 250–3,000 Savage rifle he had recently purchased. Furthermore, he said he would like to see how it could take down something like a big wolf or a mountain lion.

Before that winter was over, Trapper Garner got his wish. Chancing upon a pack of wolves feeding on the carcass of a two year-old steer, Garner took aim and put a bullet through the mid-section of the lead wolf of the pack. The bullet hit the animal a little too far back to be a killing shot. Since it hit the animal in the paunch area, it could not have the destructive effect of a lung or a shoulder shot. Accompanied by their wounded leader, the pack turned and were gone from sight before Garner could get another shot fired. Most animals would eventually have died from the type of wound the big wolf was given—except for a very large timber wolf. In fact, even this big guy might have died if it were not for the fraternity of the pack; they never deserted him. Traveling when he could travel, the pack rested when he was too sick to go on. While he trailed the pack, Garner saw signs that they were sticking by their leader. They killed one or two beef every day. Presumably, the wounded would feed on the warm blood to keep up his strength. After several days of trailing and reading signs, Garner gave up the chase. It was clear the wounded wolf was getting stronger every day. There had been no glimpse of the pack since the day Garner shot their leader. The next year during deer season, a man by the name of Sam Royer of Norwood said he shot nearly a whole box of shells at a pack of wolves in Burn Draw, which is about five miles east of Dry Creek Basin. One of the biggest wolves appeared to be wounded, but there was no sign of blood in their trail. Later, Sam wondered if this was the same wolf that the well-known Trapper Garner had talked about and if this animal was acting wounded from the effect of a previous rifle shot.

139

Chapter 14

A CASE OF TEMPER

When the rodeo began to be quite popular around this area, a lot of cowboys figured they could supplement their meager incomes by competing for some of the available prize money. Most cowboys got plenty of experience at riding (since that was their daily task), but the bucking horses of the Rodeo were usually very unpredictable. On any given day, the rider was likely to be presented a chance to demonstrate his talents. With the roping events, however, things were somewhat different.

At roundup time a lot of roping was done in order to complete the branding job. Each ranch's best ropers did the bulk of the roping, but all of the hands who cared to could help out. The men who handled the cattle while they were down and stretched out, during branding, earmarking, castrating, or vaccinating were called ground men. They did the hard, sweaty work, and each was skilled in their respective assignments. When the roper threw his loop on a cow to be branded, he would dally the rope around the saddle horn. Then the horse would drag the cow up to the fire where the ground men would take over. Calmly sitting and waiting until his rope was freed, the roper would return to the herd for another critter. Because it was much easier work, roping was a prized assignment. Some cowboys really disliked having to get off a horse and do any work afoot. Their high-heeled boots made walking somewhat of a chore because, after all, they were made for riding. The long, sloping heel was designed to keep the weight of the cowboy centered at the arch and to prevent his foot from going clear through the stirrup during mounting and the wild riding that was a frequent part of the job.

To be good at roping took a lot of practice. If they were to do their part expediently, the horses had to go through the routines almost daily. The cowboy and his horse needed to work together to learn to anticipate one another's moves and the moves of the cattle which they chased. The following incident is about a couple of roping cowboys who were about the best in the country; they always won money at the rodeos. For years they stayed in practice between shows by roping the cattle of their employers while they were out on the open range. The cattle should have been ranging so they could thrive and put on weight. Instead they were often chased into exhaustion. One day a violent-tempered foreman decided he had seen enough.

It was a hot day in July on the Pitchfork Ranch. A man by the name of Pat Gaines was foreman for the outfit owned by Ed Lavender. On this particular day some much-needed fence repairs were on the agenda. Now, this type of work was clearly beneath the dignity of most cowboys who took themselves seriously, and two of the best cowboys on the Pitchfork, Jay Boss and Mort Rullison, were certainly no exception. If they could do it from a horse, they would willingly do almost any kind of work. When foreman Gaines sent them out to fix fence that morning, they probably already had their day planned out. When they left and didn't take any fencing tools along with them, Gaines figured they must be up to something. What followed later that evening was a typical incident in the lives of cowboys that could have very quickly ended in bloodshed and killing.

What the two cowboys had on their minds that day was to get in a little roping practice. At the first bunch of cattle they came across, each took down their ropes, shook out a loop, and picked out a yearling on which to hone their roping skills. Going from one part of the range to another, they spent most of the day in this manner and roped quite a few head of cattle in the process.

That evening, Pat Gaines was late getting back to camp. In the bunkhouse, the cowboys were all playing poker and spinning a few yarns. Since Pat knew that this was where they would all be, he headed straight for them. Boiling with rage, he stormed into the bunkhouse and demanded to know what in the hell they thought they were doing roping cattle all day when he had specifically sent them out to fix fencelines. Mort started to say something, but Gaines' temper was completely out of control. After he jerked out his six-shooter, he knocked Mort out of his chair with it. Then, he got the drop on Jay Boss and Jack Andress, another cowboy who was also present in the bunkhouse and who had tried to come to his comrades' aid. Gaines calmed down somewhat and got control of his anger, but as soon as Mort came around enough to know what was going on, Gaines fired the two of them right then and there.

Chapter 15

THE KILLING OF INDIAN HENRY

Henry Whacker, later known as Indian Henry, was a Digger Indian from a tribe in the southwest Utah and southeast Nevada areas. The term "Digger" evolved from the habit these Indians had for digging in the ground for most of their food. When he was about seventeen years old, Henry was either abandoned by his parents or else told to get out on his own. Fortunately he was picked up along a wagon trail by a couple of families on their way to settle in the area of Paradox, Colorado. The settlers were the Dan Nyswonger family and the James Huff family, who settled in Paradox in 1879 before the Ute Indians were relocated to their reservation. Jimmy Huff adopted the Indian they had picked up along the trail, and he was known by some after that as Henry Huff. To the majority of people, however, he was called Indian Henry. The Indian received a little schooling while he finished growing up in the Paradox area. Well known and well liked in Paradox and San Miguel County, he later did cowboy work for some of the cattle outfits in the area and eventually owned a small herd of his own. He registered a stock brand on April 15, 1885, Montrose County.

After the turn of the century and the discovery of radium, uranium mining became quite an industry in the west end of Montrose County. Indian Henry staked quite a few claims in the Bull Canyon area; he worked (dug out the ore) some claims, but he mostly prospected, staked claims, and then held them for sale. Only the most high grade ore (pitchblend) could be used for the extraction of radium. It took a lot of prospecting and assaying to locate the desirable ore bodies.

The North Standard Chemical Corporation had some mines in this same part of the Bull Canyon Mining District, and the men who worked them lived in a boarding house built in the bottom of Bull Canyon, very near the wash caused by the rushing waters of the spring run-off. The boarding house was managed by John Keske, whose wife took in all the miners' washing and did their cooking. There was also a shelter under the overhanging rims for the pack burros and saddle horses. (The remains of both the old boarding house and the animal shelter are still visible today.) Indian Henry used to spend quite a bit of time around the boarding house; it gave him a chance to visit with people, but, mostly, he loved to play Hearts, a card game that he played with Keske. Indian Henry, who had reportedly sold some of his claims, was thought to have quite a bit of money. Where he had it (if he had it) has never been discovered. Some people don't believe that he ever had more than just pocket change—enough for a few games of Hearts and a meal at the boarding house. John Keske however, believed very strongly that Indian Henry did have a lot of money and that he either hid it around his cabin, which was not far from the boarding house or had it stashed with some of his personal belongings in the room he used while staying with the Keskes.

On the afternoon of May 11, 1917, in the Keske Boarding House, three men sat down at the dining room table to play some Hearts. The men were Clark Akers, an old time cowboy, John Keske, and Indian Henry. John Keske had concealed a six shooter in his boot top. For that reason alone, I think the whole episode that followed was a set-up to kill Indian Henry and steal the money they thought he had. During the course of the play, Keske led an ace, and Indian Henry trumped it. Outraged at this turn of events, Keske brought up his six-shooter and shot Indian Henry square in the mouth; he was killed instantly. Later inspection of the hand held by the Indian showed a void in the suit of the ace lead. His trump was valid and proper.

The Montrose County Sheriff was notified of the killing, and Keske was lodged in the County Jail for about six months while awaiting trial. For some reason Clark Akers seemed to be afraid of John Keske and did whatever Keske told him to. During the trial, Akers and Keske both testified under oath that Indian Henry was molesting Mrs. Keske and that her husband had killed the Indian in defense of her honor. With no testimony to refute this, the Judge had no other recourse than to let John Keske go free. He left the country by way of Gunnison, Colorado, headed east and has never been heard of around this part of Colorado again.

Although Indian Henry had a lot of friends, there wasn't much they could do now. A young cowpuncher, working for an old man by the name of Tracy, probably did more than anyone else to pay tribute to a good man. After Indian Henry was buried under a huge overhanging sandstone cliff at the junction of Picket Corral Draw and Bull Canyon Wash, George Riley put up a tombstone. Carved from hard red sandstone, its lettering was laboriously chiseled out by hand. He fenced the grave area off to protect it from livestock. Still there today for anyone to see, it is marked with this simple epitaph:

HENRY HUFF
MAY 11
1917
AGE 55

My uncle, Jim Williams, who was well known all over the country as' a packer, used to pack the ore from mines in Bull Canyon. Well acquainted with Indian Henry and John Keske, he had spent many a night at the old boarding house. He had often stabled his burros under the overhanging rimrocks. After reaching the top of Monogram Mesa with a Burro pack string, he would go north across the Mesa to the Joe Dandy Tram. The ore buckets on the tram took the ore to the valley floor in East Paradox. There, the big ore wagons with six-horse teams would be loaded up, and the ore would be hauled to Placerville where it was then loaded on the train for its final destination.

Over the past few years there have been quite a few people with electronic metal detectors looking around the Bull Canyon area for the money supposedly hidden by Indian Henry. Located on a big wide bench up out of the east side of Picket Corral Draw, his cabin is a very popular spot for searching. As far as anyone knows, nothing of value has ever been found. About twenty-five years ago, two young men thought they had found something there when their metal detector located something in the shape of a long box buried several feet deep. They began digging, and struck metal, and soon exposed the corner of a steel box. After frantically digging the whole thing out, they discovered the ash box from an old time cook stove.

For many years after his death, Indian Henry's cabin was used as a cow camp by old "Tub" Tracy. Ethan Allen Tracy was his real name. He got the nickname "Tub" from the "Tub L" brand that he picked up after Billy Randall dropped it in preference for the Spectacle Brand that belonged to the outfit he bought from Harry Adsit.* The cabin was solidly constructed out of large Cottonwood logs that had been hauled up from the bottom of Bull Canyon where it enters the Dolores River Canyon. Half the cabin has a cement floor; a rock fireplace stands against the south wall. The fireplace was the sole source of heat and the place where the cooking was done. Although there was never a stove inside the cabin, there was an old stove outside

*The "Tub L" brand was made like this, ⊻

147

where water was heated for baths and washing clothes. Tracy refinished the concrete hearth and carved a big "Tub L" right in the middle before the cement had hardened. He built the picket corral as a place to trap some of his wild cattle that were difficult to gather and drive anywhere. His cow trap was in the upper end of a dead-end canyon; wide wings extended from the corral so that the cattle driven up the canyon would soon be inside the wings and then the enclosure itself before they had a chance to escape. The corral is very well concealed in the pinion and cedars; the last time I saw it (1967), it was remarkably well preserved. Built totally out of native cedar, which takes about a hundred years to rot away underground. Indian Henry's cabin is roofed over with cedar poles. At one time, it had about a foot of sod growing on top.

Another of Tracy's cow camps was a cabin down in the bottom of Wild Steer Canyon. It was here that the words, "Fly blown in Wild Steer," were written on the wall of the cabin by some disgusted cowboy. In 1938, I stayed a couple of days in this cabin, while helping Clarence Hosley round up his cattle off Skein Mesa. We also had to gather cattle from Wild Steer Mesa and bring the entire bunch up over Monogram Mesa. Over the next few days we would trail out of the head of Bull Canyon (over the same trail my Uncle Jim had so many times followed) and up to the ranch in Dry Creek Basin.

Chapter 16

THE SAN MIGUEL DEVELOPMENT CORPORATION

One That Failed

Water was so important. Starting after 1900, irrigation schemes sprang up all over the San Miguel Basin. Almost any stream that wasn't over-decreed already would suddenly become the focal point of some development plan to store it and dispense it through canals and ditches. On August 27, 1908, a man from Colorado Springs by the name of Duncan Chisholm owned a survey that called for bringing water out of the San Miguel River Canyon a few miles northwest of Norwood. It was yet another scheme to put water in Mailbox Park. When completed, the canal would furnish irrigation water not only to Mailbox Park but all the way to East Paradox. Four hundred cubic feet per second was to be the capacity of the canal. Since it was going to be constructed on a steep, brushy, rock-bound canyon side that was plagued with heavy cloudburst rains several times each summer, the canal would have to follow this canyon side for seventeen miles before it reached a point where a 460 foot tunnel would actually bring the water out of the canyon. Also, there had to be twenty miles of flume because of the many rims to negotiate and the many small canyons to cross from Coventry to East Paradox. Chisholm got Buckley Wells, a wealthy mine owner from Telluride, interested in putting up the money to pioneer the survey through to the tunnel site. Robert McF. Doble was hired as the engineer, and work on the right-of-way was started that same year. After incorporating these men called their company The San Miguel Development Company. The company's headquarters was on the land later known as the Perry Michelson ranch.

Carved out of the hillside from Saltado Creek for about eight miles, the trail can be plainly seen today from the highway along the San Miguel River. All of the blasting and work that was done to construct the new Norwood Hill Road obliterated that part of the trail as well as the old road that used to be the stage coach route onto Wrights' Mesa. The survey called for $150,000 to complete the system; that was considered very expensive for the time, because other systems were being completed for $20,000 to $30,000. Three years into construction, the project was cancelled due to lack of funds.

The owners of the company still wanted to be in the water and land development business, so the two Nelson Reservoirs in Main Beaver were bought as well as the Mailbox extension of the Nelson Ditch. By using the existing Naturita Canal system to transport water and then by putting it into the Nelson Ditch, the water eventually would flow into the Mailbox Extension. Here, terrain problems caused the canal to be brought south toward Maverick Draw. There, in the vicinity of Hook Draw, in 1911, The San Miguel Development Corporation built a wooden flume across Maverick Draw. After crossing the draw, a ditch was constructed to take the water to a site where it was again dumped into the Naturita Canal (now the Gurley canal). This piece of construction was called the Coventry Lateral. To carry the extra flow for several miles to a point where it was taken out again, an enlargement had to be made to the Naturita Canal. This was where the canal would begin that would actually deliver water to Mailbox Park.

The San Miguel Development Corporation was running out of money again. The infusion of capitol received from some eastern investors, after abandoning the San Miguel Project, was not sufficient for the owners' plans. Irrigation projects in the San Miguel Basin don't all produce solid, reliable and profitable organizations. If the San Miguel Development Corporation could have foreseen the problems with the San Miguel Project and had used the money that Buckley Wells invested to help build the Mailbox Park System instead, things would have worked out very differently for this company.

Chapter 17

THE HISTORY OF THE MAMMOTH RESERVOIR OUTLET DITCH

Also Known as the Redlands Canal and the Jap Ditch

The "Jap Ditch" as it was called during the late 1920s and early 1930s had the potential of being a great irrigation scheme. The water rights were good and had the possibility of being improved. However, the ditch would have to negotiate a canyonside for five miles. Mudslides, falling rocks, and heavy rains wreak havoc on canyonside ditches. Also, the twenty to thirty foot high rims would cause the need for an enormous amount of flume.

The original Mammoth Reservoir Survey and the Beaver-Naturita Intake Canal were the work of Sam Spradlin of Nucla, Colorado. Water for the Mammoth Reservoir was to be obtained by filing for a decree out of West Beaver Creek. By enlarging the Naturita Intake Canal, the water would be transported to a point where a headgate would discharge it into the proposed Beaver-Naturita Intake Canal. This canal would empty in turn into Brewster Creek which would flow to a point where continuation of the Beaver Intake Canal would carry the water in a westerly direction out through Nelson Gap and to the drainage of Middle Naturita Creek. The Mammoth Reservoir was to be constructed in this drainage. In later years, The Lilylands Development Company used this same survey for its east extension. Had the company completed the canal for the water out of Fall Creek, the rest of the Beaver-Naturita Intake System would have been used.

Even though the Gurley Ditch and the Lone Cone Ditch were already in operation, there were still thirty-five hundred acres on the lower end of Wrights' Mesa that needed another system. Although it was a very large undertaking for one man, the rewards would be great after completion. Perhaps Mr. Guy decided to try the outlet ditch first; if everything went well then the reservoir could come later. The outlet ditch would follow its natural course in Naturita Canyon until it reached a point in the southwest corner of Section seventeen, Township forty-five, Rangeline Thirteen W. Here the construction would have to begin.

At that time, there were two camps of Japanese laborers in Naturita Canyon; A.E. Guy recruited about thirty or forty of them. With teams, scrapers, and plows, as well as a lot of hand labor, the construction was underway. When they reached the first rimrock, the construction of the flumes began. Instead of using length of pipe, the flumes were built from three foot wide by twelve foot long sheets of galvanized roofing of about twenty-eight gauge thickness. The trestle that supported the flume was constructed like other trestles built to support tremendous weight. Ten feet apart, the top timbers served as the sides of the flume as well as the anchor point for the ends of the steel sheets that had been formed into a sort of flattened half-circle. Each sheet was supported underneath by two steel bands that fit into a pre-formed groove on each side of the sheet. These steel bands were then secured to the ends of timbers that were laid across the flume. Because the sheets overlapped each other by a few inches, this space was filled with burlap and tar to form

One of the many flumes in the troubled "Jap Ditch." (Courtesy of the Naturita Colorado Historical Museum.)

a tight seal. Although it was thought that the weight of the water would complete the water-tight seal, time would soon reveal the serious flaws in this construction method. A catwalk was built along the side of the trestle for the men to work from and later for the flume walker to travel on during daily inspections.

It soon became clear that the steel bands holding the flume weren't strong enough to support the weight of the water. With the flume running at capacity, this weight would have been three and one-half tons per each linear foot of flume. A bit of arithmetic will show that a section of flume one hundred feet long would weigh 336 tons when full of water. Small wonder that, when leaks developed and the support for the timbers washed away, large sections of the flume came crashing down. Also, overhanging rocks that broke loose and fell onto the flume caused sections of the flume to drop away as well. The resulting washout meant weeks of repair.

The water had to be turned back to the creek each time repairs had to be made; then it would be redirected into the system once again for another try. The expense of the upkeep of the poorly designed and badly constructed flumes was the major reason for the abandonment of the project. The ditch was surveyed to be 17.21 miles long. Built on a grade of thirteen feet to the mile, it was designed to carry 112 cfs. Mr. Guy only built the ditch as far as his ranch (now the lower Alexander Ranch). If the rest of the system had been built, it would have been called the Redlands Canal. Construction at the ranch was completed in 1913 at a cost of $20,000. Under the Carey Act of 1894, Federal funding was available for irrigation projects such as this.

The Lone Cone Ditch and Reservoir Company had completed its system by this time and claimed Naturita creek at its headquarters by being the first company to put it to beneficial use. The water sources that remained for the Mammoth Resevoir Outlet Ditch were the streams of Log Corral Gulch, Reservoir Creek, and the early runoff from the land surrounding the Mammoth Reservoir site.

The Mammoth Reservoir was never built under that name. The Colorado Department of Game & Fish became interested in the site. After a lengthy study of the runoff from Naturita Creek, it was determined that it could fill a fairly large reservoir. The original Mammoth Reservoir was surveyed for a capacity of 12,000 acre-feet. A.E. Guy, who owned the Bank in Norwood, owned the survey and probably had some serious thoughts about constructing the reservoir. He filed on a four cubic feet per second (cfs.) reservoir decree out of Middle Naturita Creek and Bennet Creek and constructed a ditch to carry that decree to the reservoir site. Shortly after 1960, the Game and Fish Department began constructing a reservoir on this site and called it Miramonte Reservoir.

An interesting side-note here is that when the Game and Fish Department began the Miramonte Project, William (Bill) Bray happened by there one day while a party of surveyors was starting to survey for the Miramonte Intake Canal. While stopping to chat for awhile, Bill learned the nature of their survey and told them that there was already a surveyed ditch there. Bill told them of his Uncle, A.E. Guy, and his plans for the Mammoth Reservoir. Since the surveyors found this a little suspect, Bill drove back to Redvale and produced the original blueprints with the elevations and headgate locations exactly as the new survey called for. The old ditch was easily found, which considerably aided the construction of the new one. Built to the same capacity that was called for in the Mammoth Survey, Miramonte Reservoir was completed and dedicated in 1963.

A.E. Guy's "Jap Ditch" was used for many years. Henry Darling was the flume walker or ditch rider, as they were also called; he used to keep himself in fresh fish by hanging gunny sacks in the headgates. Irrigation schemes were blossoming all around the San Miguel Basin. Almost before the survey on Mammoth Reservoir was completed, a group of men filed an enlargement on it with plans to take a canal to the Lilylands. I guess the old saying that "hope springs eternal" was certainly true in this case.

Chapter 18

THE LILYLANDS DEVELOPMENT COMPANY

One That Succeeded

After the Naturita Ditch Company failed to extend its canals to the West Lilylands, a group of inspired men with financial connections formed what was called the Lilylands Development Company. They sold water certificates in a proposed reservoir and canal system to people interested in buying land. Since there were plenty of buyers for the water, all the certificates were soon sold. Water had been appropriated from streams on the north and west sides of the Lone Cone Mountain. The survey, which was owned by Clarence Wood of Coventry, Colorado, was completed in 1905 by Henry Spradlin, and the reservoir site was surveyed the same year. Construction could now begin.

During the winter, before the actual construction began, several area men with teams and wagons, hauled loads of coal and dumped them along the right of way so the big steam-powered shovel would have a ready supply of fuel as it dug its way along. The reservoir was not built at the start of construction. Instead, the canal was dug from a point where the West Naturita and Spectacle Creek converged to the West Lilylands. Then, the power shovel was moved back to the Lone Cone area, and the east extension was dug; this would bring water from Brewster Creek and Naturita Creek as it meandered its way around the base of the Lone Cone. Although there was no reservoir, a wide shallow draw that the canal ran through looked as if it could be made to hold quite a bit of water upon construction of a dam at the lower end. (It was only after the ditch had been in operation for about twenty years, that this dam was finally constructed.) A trench was dug across the draw, and tall strong cedar posts were set in the trench as close together as they could be crowded in. After the trench was filled and tamped tight with dirt, more dirt was piled up against the cedars; an outlet gate was also devised. With this primitive dam, the wide shallow draw served as the only storage area for many years.

Down in the Lilylands (both east and west) the farmers had put the water to good use. Excellent crops of alfalfa were raised. Some farms yielded as much as five tons per acre for the season. Small grains did real well, too. Almost anything planted produced bumper crops. However, dark clouds were forming on the heretofore, bright blue horizon. Operating with barely any storage was very risky, but reservoirs cost a lot of money. On top of not having a proper storage facility, a part of the canal had begun to leak through the bottom. About a quarter of a mile of the ditch had originally been blasted out of pure rimrock where the grade brought it out of Broad Canyon. Because the blasting had weakened the deep formation, the water had begun to find its way down through the many cracks that had been formed. Today, this would not constitute much of a problem due to modern machinery and methods like drilling and grouting the cracks. Back then, however, money and lack of equipment made it a very big problem. Also, around the beginning of the 1930s, it was rumored that the officers of the Lilylands Corporation had sold the main water rights supplying the east extension to The Lone Cone Ditch and Reservoir company. As it turned out, this was a killing blow to the water-users of the Lilylands. The holders of the corporate gold bonds and the officers of the Lilylands Development Corporation decided that for about the same amount of money it would take to build a reservoir, they could appropriate water out of Fall Creek. By constructing the canal surveyed by W. H. Nelson in 1905, they could bring the water into the Naturita Beaver Extension canal. By enlarging the canal, their water could be transported to a point where a headgate would discharge it into yet another canal. In turn, this would cause the flow to empty into Brewster Creek and from there to their own east extension.

The officers went ahead with their plan, and the canal out of Fall Creek was about 90 per cent complete when the company ran out of money. The construction methods were rather unorthodox—about a mile or so of the canal would be completed and then a quarter of a mile would be skipped and another quarter done. This pattern was followed throughout the length of the canal. Whatever end this means justified is not known for sure, but what is known is that the construction ceased abruptly. Another grand scheme was down the drain. If they still had the water from the east extension flowing into the system and had been able to stop the water loss from seepage, the farmers in the Lilylands could probably have gotten along fine. They really didn't have a chance though. In an effort to raise more money, the bond holders started pressuring the farmers to exchange their water certificates for corporate gold bonds at a considerably higher rate of exchange. Most of the farmers didn't have the money. The ones who did had lost all faith in the corporation's management who had sold the water rights for the east extension to finance the Fall Creek Canal, a project which was later abandoned as a partially completed ditch at best. The east extension had cost a lot of money; now it was a white elephant. To the farmers in the Lilylands, resurrecting the canal system looked like an exercise in futility. One by one they packed up and left, sold what they could, and took with them what couldn't be sold.

About ten miles to the south of the Lilylands area, lies a huge area of prime farming and ranching land known as Dry Creek Basin. For years, at least sixty square miles of tillable land had just been sitting and begging for people to settle it. It was all Government land, but there were scattered homesteads all over it. Years of waiting for water that didn't come had caused a lot of people to give up and leave. When the Great Depression hit, this caused more settlers to leave the area. This area had been bypassed by the Lilylands Canal group in their rush to reach the development. Now there was an awful lot of land available just for taxes. This didn't pose much of a problem for those with financial connections. The depression was on, and the banks had most of the money, but some was available to certain people. The wiser ones used the credit and bought up vast acreages.

The CCC Camp, which was built in Dry Creek Basin, brought in quite a few people who bought property because they wanted to stay. About this same time Dan Hughes Sr. of Montrose was buying up every available piece of property he could, particularly if it carried a winter grazing permit. He had been running sheep in this area for years, and he knew exactly the parcels of land that he wanted to buy. With eight or nine Dry Creek Basin ranchers behind him financially, he went to the bondholders of the Lilylands Development Corporation and offered them a lump sum for the corporation—lock, stock, and barrel. The bondholders jumped at the chance to unload what had been a burden for several years, and the group of ranchers became the new owners of the canal system. As expected, they didn't send any water past Dry Creek Basin. Constant improvements to the ditch and the construction of the new 500 acre-foot Lilylands Reservoir (built by the Hughes Brothers) made a

160

tremendous improvement in water delivery to the farming areas of Dry Creek Basin.

The sons of Dan Hughes Sr. continued to operate the Dry Creek Basin ranches and continued buying land and water at every opportunity. They filed on the water out of Fall Creek and completed the old Lilylands-Fall Creek Extension. Instead of connecting the canal with the Naturita-Beaver Extension, though, they crossed Saltado Creek and built a canal to the land that they owned on Beaver Mesa. This ability to irrigate the pasture lands increased their carrying capacity tenfold and resulted in an end-product of more and bigger lambs at shipping time.

Chapter 19

THE OUTLAW ED WILLIAMS

The Good and the Bad

A cowboy by the name of Lawrence Hankins had homesteaded in 1915 in the lower end of Big Gypsum Valley and was spending the winter there looking after a bunch of "Pitchfork"* steers (cattle belonging to Ed Lavender). Hankins had been suffering with a bad cold for quite awhile, and it eventually turned into pneumonia. Ed Williams, who had also taken up a homestead not far away, along the Dolores River, happened by on a day that Hankins was too sick to get out of bed. When Ed saw how bad off Lawrence was, he reassured him that everything was going to be all right and that he was going to help. Even though it was late in the evening, Ed mounted his horse and started for the closest doctor. Because there was close to a foot of snow on the ground, it made pretty tough going for the horse. Making progress as good as the mount was capable of, Ed pushed on. By about midnight, the horse was getting pretty weary, so Ed rode into the ranch of George Young where he borrowed a fresh horse, leaving his tired horse until his eventual return. From there Mr. Williams cut across country in the general direction of Redvale in the hopes of finding the old Indian Trail, across

---

* The "Pitchfork" brand was made like this, ⼁ .

Naturita Canyon, below Shenandoah. Knowing the country like his own back yard, he was on the trail after just a few hours of steady riding. Before long he had climbed out of the canyon and was headed towards the Bement Ranch a little east of Redvale. It was nearing daylight when he rode into the yard and put his horse away in the barn. Lawrence Hankins was married to a Bement girl, so Ed felt that this was the most proper place to go for help. After waking the sleeping family, he asked to use the telephone. He called Dr. Bollinger in Norwood and explained the situation and the location of the patient. Dr. Bollinger started out immediately. At the Bement Ranch, Ed got in with the doctor, and they drove to the cabin in Big Gyp Valley. Staying about half a day, Dr. Bollinger cared for and watched over Lawrence Hankins until the crisis had passed. After leaving medicine and instructions with the patient, Dr. Bollinger went back to Norwood in company of Ed Williams. Ed rode as far as the Bement Ranch where he saddled his borrowed horse and started for the Young Ranch in Dry Creek Basin. With a general thanks to the gracious people who had loaned him the fresh horse, he caught his own mount and started out on the last twenty mile leg of the long, grueling trip back to his own cabin along the Dolores River.

Somebody had been leaving his gates open, and if anything would make Ed Williams mad (or any other stockman for that matter), that was it. Asking around for information about those who had been going through his gates, he finally narrowed it down to a couple of people. Gates are actually just a movable part of a fence, and a fence is put up to either keep something in or to keep something out. When a closed gate is intentionally left open, that destroys its purpose. Ed Williams was having to do a lot of unnecessary riding to keep his cattle at home and to keep other cattle where they belonged. One day, he decided to have a talk with the people he figured were guilty of leaving his gates open. He caught his horse, saddled up, and rode to the home of

Dick Freel, who lived not too far away. Ed Williams rarely went anywhere without his trusty Luger (a German pistol from World War I), and he had it with him on this day. Dick Freel didn't seem to want to exchange pleasantries and stopped Ed quite a ways from the door of the house. "What's the nature of your business?" said Freel.

Williams replied, "I'm looking for the scoundrel who's been leaving my gates down." Accusations were launched, and a few colorful character descriptions were exchanged. This led to some references as to ancestry and pedigree and a few more unpleasant things being tossed back and forth.

Apparently deciding the conversation had gone on long enough, Dick Freel reached behind the door and came up with a rifle. At this turn of events Ed reached behind his belt for the old Luger. After a couple of shots the Luger jammed and wouldn't load or fire. Every time Freel would show his gun to take a shot, Ed would run in a ziz-zag pattern toward the cabin. Sounds crazy to charge a fortified location with a jammed pistol, but to turn and run would have meant certain death. Freel may not have known that Ed's gun wouldn't fire. After a few more shots from the house were fired, Ed made it up to the door and jumped inside. Just as he did, Freel shoved the rifle barrel toward his mid-section and pulled the trigger. A split instant before the gun could fire, Ed jammed down on the barrel with both hands— hard and fast. By the time the gun actually fired, it was pointed in the general direction of Ed's left knee. The bullet made a considerable flesh wound. In telling about it afterward, Ed said he was certain he was "gut shot." Before Dick Freel could reload his gun, Ed wrestled him to the floor. After disarming him though, he declined the option of killing him. After all, he had come up there to talk. After he helped Freel to his feet, and they talked things over sensibly, Williams got on his horse and headed back to his homestead. Several people asked Ed if he had any trouble with the healing of the bullet wound. "Naw," he replied, "I just took the old ramrod with a cleaning patch soaked in iodine and ran it back and forth through the wound a few times. It healed up just fine."

A colorful character who had been in more than a few shooting scrapes, Ed Williams had the reputation of being just a little bit bad. To some people he was a gunman and a suspected cattle rustler. Probably the worst thing that he ever did was when he took up his homestead along the Dolores River and fenced Ed Lavender's cattle off from their favorite drinking place. Lavender was the biggest cattleman in the area at this time and didn't take kindly to having his cattle fenced away from water. When Mr. Lavender tried to get Ed Williams to sell the place to him, he offered him better than going prices, but Ed Williams had settled there because he liked the place. That was where Williams intended to stay.

Ed Lavender knew a lot of ways to remove stubborn obstacles, and it wasn't long before Williams was arrested on a warrant served out of Monticello, Utah. Mr. Williams had gone to Telluride, to the County Commissioner's Office, to collect the bounty on a half-dozen wolf scalps when Sheriff Pilcher tapped him on the shoulder and served him with the warrant for cattle rustling. This seems like a rather bogus accusation to come out of an area, that, for forty years or more, had the reputation of being a place where the only time a man ate his own beef was when he had a meal with the neighbors. Brought to trial on January 26, 1926, Ed Williams was found guilty as charged after a lengthy trial. Ed's attorney, Merle Vincent, filed for a new trial and a stay of sentencing. When this was granted, Mr. Williams posted bond of $1,500 and returned to his home in Gypsum Valley. A new trial date was set, but through a misunderstanding, Williams failed to be on hand when his new trial started. He was on his way to Montrose, when he learned he was going to be late for his trial. Advised by his friends not to continue and informed of the serious illness of his common-law wife, he returned to his ranch.

Montrose County sheriff, H. C. Getty and his son left Montrose on a Tuesday night for the west end of the county. A $1000 reward had been posted by the County Commissioners for the apprehension of Ed Williams, and these men intended to collect it. After they drove into the Disappointment country, they worked their way down to the Williams ranch. Herman Getty said they spent several days in the Gypsum Valley region trying to locate Williams but were unable to do so. At about 2:30 A.M. Sunday, the two Gettys, John Lavender and Dick Freel, who had been deputized for this special occasion, started out from the Freel ranch. They went to the Williams ranch a mile or so away. The two Gettys went down to the house as close as they could get and hid in the willows along the river. Dick Freel and John Lavender were to take their places at the other corners of the house as close as they could get in. They all waited. The dogs barked but didn't come down to where the Gettys were hiding. About 9:30 A.M., young Getty came over to where his dad was hiding and said he didn't think it was any use; Ed wasn't home. The sheriff said he thought he was home because, when Mrs. Dolan went out to milk the cow, someone had started a fire. Sheriff Getty said they would leave if Williams didn't show by 10:00 A.M. At 10:00 A.M. exactly, Williams came out and went over to an outbuilding. As he walked out of the house, Getty had a good shot at him in the back, but he didn't want to shoot him that way. As Williams was on his way back to the house, Getty, who was within fifty or sixty yards of Williams, commanded him to "stick 'em up!" Williams didn't do that. Instead, he jumped sideways several steps behind a big cotton wood tree about three feet in diameter. In the confidence of friends, Ed Williams had sworn that he would never surrender or be taken alive, especially by the "Pitchfork Posse" (some of Ed Lavender's cowboys who regularly swooped down on Williams and tried to capture him). At the command "stick 'em up," the first thought to go through Williams' mind was that the "Pitchfork" outfit was after him again. If Sheriff Getty had identified himself by saying, "Sheriff Getty of Montrose; stick 'em up," perhaps things would have turned out differently for all concerned. Ed pulled his Luger from his belt and started shooting.

As he fired he yelled, "Babe, bring out the Winchesters." Mrs. Dolan soon came out with two Winchesters and took her place behind the tree.

The Gettys could hear her say, "A little higher, Ed; a little lower, Ed; to the right, Ed," as she directed him how to aim. She must have also loaded the guns for him as he shot as fast as he could at Getty and his son. Heman, Jr. tried to work his way farther around to one side to get a better shot at Williams. Finally, the firing stopped from his father's outpost. He wondered if his dad had been killed or what had happened. After young Herman worked his way around to the river and after he got a good look at his father, he found that Mrs. Dolan had gone down there and was giving his dad first aid. She shouted up to Herman to throw down his gun and come down and help care for the sheriff. There was nothing else left to do. Presently, Williams came down with some sheets, and they tore the sheets into bandages and bound up Getty's wound as best they could.

During this time Williams tried to make conversation and said, "You were putting them in pretty close."

To that, Sheriff Getty replied, "That old tree was just too much protection, I couldn't get a clear shot at you." A truck belonging to Sullivan Brothers was borrowed, and Williams brought out a mattress and a set of bed springs. He placed them in the truck and helped make Getty as comfortable as possible. At this time John Lavender mounted his horse and rode about fifteen miles, cross country to the community of Cedar, where he had the use of a telephone at the home of Ronald Mair. He called the Montrose Sheriff's office and told them of the wounding of Getty. The injured sheriff was being transported to Norwood and would need a very good doctor and an ambulance. Dick Freel returned to his home which was only about two miles away.

The truck carrying Sullivan, H.C. Getty and Getty's son, arrived in Norwood at about 11:00 P.M. Sunday. Getty suffered a great deal from loss of blood and shock. At Norwood, physicians gave Getty first aid. A few hours after their arrival, Dr. Hadley, who had been sent over from Montrose with the Pond ambulance, arrived at the Norwood Clinic. That was about 5:15 A.M. Monday.

Missing the bone and the large artery that supplies the lower leg with blood, the bullet had entered the lower buttock on Getty's left side and exited down through the upper thigh. Circulation was not greatly impaired even though there had been tremendous damage to the muscle structure. Made by a softnose hunting bullet, the exit hole was almost four inches in diameter. The greatest danger now would be infection. Getty was transported to the Montrose Hospital as soon as his condition was stabilized.

Earlier, during the time that Sheriff Getty first started talking about going over to the Disappointment country to pick up Ed Williams, the "Badman of the West End" (or "Gunman" and "Rustler" as he had come to be called by the local press), friends of Getty kept telling him that if he went messing around over there he could get his rear-end shot off. From his hospital bed, Sheriff Getty jokingly admitted that the prophesy of his friends had painfully come true. However, the terrible wound that Getty received should never have happened. Regardless of what conditions developed, he had strategically placed two men in positions of control. When Williams had jumped behind the Cottonwood tree and started shooting, Getty had shouted to Freel and Lavender to get busy and shoot. They could easily have "nailed Williams to the cross." No one remembers hearing

Freel or Lavender fire a shot; just why they didn't shoot is a mystery. Had they fired at Williams, he surely would have been wounded or killed or been obliged to give up. There were four armed men around him in opposite directions, so that he would have been in a line of cross fire from four corners. Perhaps Freel remembered at that moment that Ed Williams had, on another day, spared *his* life when he could have just as easily killed him and been justified in doing so. John Lavender may have also recalled a situation about five years before when he had pulled a trigger and put a bullet into a man he really didn't intend to kill. The day he shot Baley Hurd, he wasn't shooting to kill; he was probably thinking that a one-armed Baley would be much easier to handle. He had never intended to end the man's life, and, on this day, he had no *real* reason to kill Ed Williams.

Hiding behind trees as he did, with the two Gettys out in the open, Williams had the best of it; especially since help did not come from the other corners. It is said that the shots fired by the Gettys peeled most of the bark off the tree behind which Williams was hiding. When the Gettys left, Williams made them leave their shooting irons with him.

The men could have shot Mrs. Dolan but they didn't want to do that either; her part in the shooting did make her an accessory and meant certain incarceration. The Telluride sheriff did finally pick her up one day and locked her in the County Jail. As soon as Ed heard where she was being held, he and some friends broke her out in the middle of the night, and they were not heard of again for about eighteen months. Their longing to see their children was their downfall. After traveling over five or six western states and working here and there for enough money to travel on, they finally wound up in New Castle, Colorado where the children were staying with their grandparents. Neighbors in the area reported to the sheriff that they had seen someone sneaking around the grandparents' house at night. The sheriff immediately went to search a camp ground along the

Colorado River and found Ed Williams and his common-law wife, Mrs. Dolan. Arrested peacefully, they were lodged in the Mesa County Jail in Grand Junction. For some reason, Mrs. Dolan was released; she and the children were cast adrift without anyone to care for them. Sadly, there was soon to be another child in this broken family because Mrs. Dolan was pregnant again.

Since Ed Williams had earlier been found guilty of cattle rustling (on the slim evidence of a handwriting expert), all that remained was his sentencing which was done on July 8, 1927. The judge gave him six to eight years in the Canon City Prison, with time off for good behavior. Ed served four years and made them very productive ones indeed. He learned to be a stone mason and learned about mortar and plastering. While in Canon City Prison he also learned how to inlay silver and other precious metals onto steel and became very skilled at this. After his release from prison, he returned to Norwood where he built many rock foundations for buildings in the town. His new skill as a great silversmith got him a lot of work as well. Anyone who has a pair of spurs or a bridle bit that were silver inlaid by Ed Williams has a souvenir worthy of a showplace.

Chapter 20

THE WILD CATTLE OF THE CLUB RANGE

There were many large cattle outfits operating on Wright's Mesa and neighboring areas in the years between 1880 and 1915. These outfits would spring up almost overnight and sometimes lasted about as long. Most of the ranches were named after the brand they ran or sometimes after the name of the owner. When a ranch was sold, there was usually a new brand to take over. In a few years, people were comfortable calling the ranch by a new name. Sometimes, though, a name would just seem to stick; no matter how many times the ranch sold and the brand changed to something else, the original name would outlast all others. One of the most notable ranches to retain its original identity throughout the many times that it was sold was the Club Ranch. Although the Club Ranch was sold at least eight times before 1945, and every owner used a different brand, the name Club Ranch was adopted by everyone who bought the operation. The old Club Ranch is now owned by Union Carbide Corporation. Along the bench above the river where there used to be about 115 acres of hay ground, is an area covered with settling ponds used by the Uravan mill to help stop the pollution of the San Miguel River, which flows right through there.

First owned by the San Miguel Cattle Company, the original Club Ranch was started as the result of the efforts by a retired Army doctor and some friends whom he had back East. After starting the Club Ranch on a large level bench of land above the San Miguel River at the mouth of Atkinson Creek, they set about stocking the range land around it with cattle. Made like the club suit in a card deck, the Club brand originally came from Texas. A trail herd of cattle with this brand was purchased by the San Miguel Cattle Company to stock their range. To save time re-branding all of the cattle and having them marked up by several brands, the Club brand was transferred to the new owners. Because they planned to run about 3,500 head of cattle, the first few years of the operation entailed more or less building up the herd numbers. This is where I believe the wild cattle got their beginning. While the operation was in the growth phase, insufficient attention was given to the cattle. During this time the cattle were only gathered twice a year to be cut for beef and to have the calves branded. Also, the range that was to be populated with cattle was adjacent to the area where a band of Ute Indians had stampeded a herd of cattle in 1879. This herd was owned by a man by the name of Fred Mayall, who was trying to run cattle in Paradox Valley two years before the Indians were removed; they wouldn't stand for it. The Indians had been pushed around a lot during a span of six years (1875–1881), and they were getting plenty angry at the encroachment of the White Man into their territory. At the time of this stampede, Mayall and his cowboys were forced by the Utes to eat grass like cattle and then were beaten and made to leave the area. Fred Mayall never saw his cattle again.

An episode at Burnt Cabin Springs on Cedar Point near the upper drainage of Montezuma Creek is another example of how the Utes were feeling; two men were killed, and the cabin was left to burn. During a chase after the marauding Indians, another man died from bullet wounds. In the Norwood area, Edwin Joseph was burned out twice while he was away from his home

174

on business. Joseph had settled near the springs the Utes had always used while crossing through the country on hunting trips. In the head of Disappointment Creek, two men, William Souther and James Nix, had built a cabin and laid in a winter supply of groceries with the intention of running a trap-line that winter. They returned to the cabin one afternoon and found their cabin burned to the ground. The men had to travel to Montrose (about eighty-five miles away) with their pack horses, get another supply of groceries, and build another cabin in which to spend the winter. The Indians were obviously trying to discourage the White Man from settling in their territory. Fred Mayall was probably pretty lucky to have only been beaten and sent away with the lingering taste of grass in his mouth. Usually when the Utes captured a white man, they were less than merciful. The loss of the cattle was actually a small matter.

After Mayall's cattle were stampeded into the hills, it's almost a sure bet that some of them went wild and were never gathered by the men who took over a few years later and ran cattle in this same area. Now, a few wild cattle acting as leaders where domestic cattle are run can really influence the habits of the domestics. After twenty years of operation of the Club brand, there were about half as many wild cattle in the hills surrounding the ranch as there were of the easily gathered, gentler, domestic cattle. Another factor explaining the large numbers of cattle gone wild was the questionable quality of the available cattle purchased for restocking purposes. Many of these animals were "renegades," "hideouts," and "culls" that were castaways from other operating outfits because they were too hard to gather from the open range.

The doctor, who was president of the Club Ranch outfit, died in 1884, and one of the partners from back East was subsequently elected president. The easterner then hired a general manager by the name of C.E. Wetzel from the Denver Union Stockyards. On April 15, 1885, brand recording with the

State of Colorado began; on September 22, 1885, the Club brand was recorded to the San Miguel Cattle Company. This was also the last year that the Club brand was used as a cattle brand at this outfit. The Club brand continued to be used as a horse brand, however, for many more years. In April of 1886, Ed Wetzel recorded the ∨ I ∧ brand to the San Miguel Cattle Company. For the next twenty-two years, this was the principal cattle brand that he used. During the time that Wetzel managed the Club outfit, he registered eight more brands under his name mainly because he was afraid of people working over the ∨ I ∧ brand into something that could be claimed. Wetzel recorded just about every possible brand that could be configured from the ∨ I ∧ brand, in the hope that it would stop any possibilities of cattle rustling. The location of the brand on the animal was also changed from the left ribs to the hip-side-shoulder arrangement. This was prompted by the recent rapid growth of a neighboring cattle herd whose owners were branding an ✕ ⱀ ✕ on the left ribs of their stock.

During the ten years he patented most of the land in his name under the Homestead Act, Ed Wetzel didn't draw any wages. Also, about half of the cattle had gone wild by now and couldn't be gathered. When the owners were faced with the realization that Wetzel held the winning hand in this game of cards, they gave him the Club outfit to square off their indebtedness to him. As its new owner, Wetzel continued to operate the Club outfit for about the next two years.

In 1906, a man by the name of Alexander Calhoun and his partner, named Bill Selby, came down from the Telluride area to look over the Club Ranch with the idea of purchasing it. Bill Selby was a wealthy Easterner and was interested in investing in a western cattle ranch. Mr. Calhoun liked the lay of the outfit and decided it would be a good business venture. When approached about selling out, Wetzel was enthusiastic so they got together and started making up the sale contract. Mr. Calhoun wasn't at all interested in buying cattle that were hidden in the brush, and Wetzel wasn't able to get a reliable count of them anyway. Since they couldn't be gathered by ordinary means (many even by heroic means), there just was no reasonable way to get an accurate tally on them. Mr. Calhoun proposed to buy the outfit based on the tally of the calves branded that spring, and a mother was counted for each calf. This figure was then multiplied by three to cover the yearlings and two year-olds and dry cows; the bulls that could be counted were then added to this total. There was usually only about a fifty percent calf crop where the breeding and calving are both done out on the range. Agreeing to sell under these terms, Mr. Wetzel probably knew that he was giving away an awful lot of cattle. I imagine that Calhoun had looked the ranch over enough to know that he was buying almost two for one because of the large number of mavericks and the older wild cattle that were ranging back in the hills.

As soon as Calhoun had attained possession of the Club Ranch, he began making plans to gather the wild cattle. The first thing that Calhoun wanted to do was to get in touch with Fred Sharp (see Chapter one, "The Chipmunk Steers"). He had heard that Sharp was just finishing up several years of work gathering the remnants of the "Chipmunk Steers" or as some called them, the "Spectacle Steers," which had been branded with the ᏫᏬ brand on the left ribs. They were a truly wild and wooly bunch of renegade cattle. Sharp and his partner, "Dewey" Greager, had worked mighty hard for several years to clean up the last of the Mexican cattle that Billy Randall had brought into the country to fatten and butcher for beef. When the last of the "Chipmunk Steers" (the last that could be rounded up, that is) were finally bought in, the two cowboys parted company. Calhoun then contacted Fred Sharp and offered him a contract to catch the wild cattle on the Club range.

While working over in the Blue Mountains of Utah, Fred

Sharp had gained quite a reputation for being able to bring wild cattle out of the rough breaks. The Carlisle outfit that Sharp had worked for in Utah had many wild cattle, and Fred had learned a full bag of tricks with respect to these creatures. During the years he worked over there, he had caught or helped to catch between three and four thousand head of cattle. Nephus Bailey, who worked at the Carlisle Ranch, said that he had seen Fred Sharp bring in as many as seven head of wild cattle at a time, all by himself. The Blue Mountains and surrounding territory were an unpredictable, harsh range; the many dry years during this time period made it so tough on newcomers that many would abandon their herds and leave the country with only the strongest of their animals. For this reason there was an ample stash of wild cattle to gather. The ranchers who had lived in the Blue Mountain area for many years knew how to graze their animals around and get to the grass and water ahead of the newcomers' cattle. Mostly, the cattle that couldn't find water or grass would die. When left to shift for themselves, a few of them would pull through some way and would become quite wild in a few years. The years that Fred Sharp spent bringing in the "Chipmunk Steers" were an added testimony to his already uncanny ability to seek out and collect the notorious wild cattle.

During one of the many visits I had with Fred Sharp, he told me of his early life and of events at the Carlisle Ranch when he was quite young. I believe that Fred was born in New Mexico but his parents moved to Colorado before he was five years old. Fred remembered that as they pulled into Animas City he raised the canvas at the back of the wagon and looked out. It was just getting good daylight, and the first thing he was able to make out was a man hanging from a limb of a cottonwood tree—not a very pretty sight for one so young. About a day behind the wagon Fred's Uncle, Hank Sharp, was coming along with the livestock. The Sharps, Abe and Hank, owned several very nice racehorses, and they gave them the very best

178

of care. A small party of Utes had been seen several times, and their actions suggested they were keeping pretty close watch on the movements of the livestock. One dark night, about three days travel west of Animas City, the Utes slipped into the camp and stole two of the best of the thoroughbreds and made off with them. The Utes were extremely fond of good horses and would go to most any means to get one. At daybreak, the horses were immediately discovered missing, and Hank Sharp started out on their trail. He detoured a little to pick up his brother, Abe, who was with his family in the wagon; then the two of them started out again in pursuit of the Indians and the stolen racehorses. After two days on the trail the Sharp brothers caught up with the party of Utes and demanded the return of their horses. The Utes were adamant that the horses belonged to them, and the white man had no claim to them. Hank pointed out the brands the horses wore and tried to explain that because the brands were theirs that made the horses theirs. Belligerently, the Utes refused to listen anymore and said they would not give the horses up. Since there were five of the Indians, they didn't think the white men would fight. They didn't know the Sharp Brothers very well or they would never have come to that conclusion. When it looked as if negotiations had broken off, and there was no other recourse, Hank drew his revolver and shot the Indian who had done all the talking, square in the face. The bullet exited out the back of the neck, just missing the spinal structure. Without any hesitation at all, two of the Indians grabbed the wounded one from either side. Quirting* his pony into a run, they made off toward the west. For two more days, the Sharps followed them and eventually separated the two Indians with the stolen horses from the two who were with the wounded one. Because it was two against two now, the Sharp brothers were

---

* A quirt is a hand-held whip, usually about two feet long and looped to the wrist. It inflicts pain on the animals for greater speed or obedience.

able to soon retrieve their horses. Although the Indians had continually mixed their trail with that of other bands of Indians, the Sharp boys could always tell when they were on the right track due to the bloody cedar bark poultices that had been worn by the wounded one and discarded along the way.

After a few more days of traveling, the Sharp party arrived at the Carlisle Ranch near what is present-day Monticello, Utah. The Sharps soon found employment with the Carlisle outfit; Hank as a cowboy and Abe as a blacksmith. By the time young Fred was ten years old, he was put in charge of the remuda (horse herd) and was respectfully considered "one of the hands." His job was to graze and keep track of all the horses and have the proper animals available to the cowboys at various times. The morning circle horses were made ready by sun-up and then they were traded at noon for the more specialized mounts used for roping and cutting. Fred came to be a very capable hand with the horses and took great pride in his work. One night on roundup, a band of renegade Utes who had breached the boundaries of their reservation, stole the entire horse herd and headed off in the general direction of Montezuma Creek. The only horses spared were the work teams and the ones that the night guard had saddled and tied near the wagon. Abandoning the roundup for the time being, everyone who could find even a work horse rode off on the trail of the Indians. The chase kept on for two days. When the cowboys reached Montezuma Creek, they had the horse herd in sight. During the two days of trailing, every cowboy encountered along the way was asked to join the chase. Alex Calhoun, one of the "Blue Mountain Cowboys" (see Chapter one, "The Chipmunk Steers") was one of the men who joined up with the Carlisles; when the pitched battle with the Indians began, he was a very active participant. This first meeting between Fred Sharp and Alex Calhoun led to a friendship that lasted their entire lives.

The Indians were led by Chiefs Posey and Old Polk. (Fred always referred to them as "Poke and Posey," a pair of trouble-makers.) As the fight with the Indians progressed, they used several deceptive tactics to get the cowboys to fire at them. One Indian hung a brightly colored blanket on a bush; then, from a concealed position, he caused it to move. The cowboys fell for the ruse; several of them fired at it. When the smoke from the black powder rifles gave away their position, a few of them were wounded by the return fire of the Indians. Fred Sharp was also taken in by the moving blanket ruse, and he partially rose from his hiding place to get a better look. An arrow was immediately discharged at him. It hit him under his shirt collar and made a nasty scratch extending down his back to its exit point at the belt of his jeans. When this frightened him so much he jumped up and ran for better cover, a rifle ball from another Indian's gun blasted his knee joint. This injury caused him to be laid up almost six months—quite an experience for a boy not yet eleven years old. The Indians appeared to be giving up the fight for the horses and slipped away to regroup behind a small hill. After a short council was held, they charged the cowboys to gain control of the horse herd once more. However, the "Blue Mountain Cowboys" were more determined than ever to repel the attack. Since their firepower was more than the Indians cared to face up to, control of the horse herd once more went to the cowboys. Riding out of rifle range the Indians taunted and jeered at the cowboys to try and get them to pursue them and possibly be lured into an ambush. The catcalls and antics of the Indians were to no avail, however, because the Carlisle bunch had already done what they had come to do. Pleased to have the horses back, they were relieved not to have lost any men. Fred, the only one seriously wounded, was laid out on a bedroll and hauled back to the ranch in a wagon.

A few years after this incident a group of ruthless men got control of the Carlisle Range and were very harsh in their dealings with the people with whom they shared the open range. They would ride right into a rancher's barnyard or corrals and drive off whatever stock there happened to be around, even the milk cows. When the owners went after their own critters, they were charged exorbitant prices to get them back. It was called a "gathering and holding charge" or a "fee for protecting the livestock from predators, man or animal." This part of Utah was quite close to the "outlaw trail" that stretched from Arizona to Montana. Furthermore, the hideout that was known as "robbers roost" was not more than a three-day ride from the ranch on a good horse. Quite a few of the outlaws going either north or south on the "trail" would stop and work awhile at the Carlisle Ranch. The men who ran the ranch were well known to a lot of men who were "on the dodge." Welcome to stop at the ranch, these men could work awhile, let their horses rest up, and get a new set of shoes. The outlaws used these opportunities to check around in case any strangers in the area might have been asking questions. If some bounty hunting sheriff was close onto an outlaw's trail, and the outlaw's horse was too leg-weary and sore-footed to travel any farther, he would simply rope a horse out of some pasture, abandon his mount, and go on. Fred told me that when the fall roundup was over and the big horse herd was not needed again until spring, they were turned out on the winter range and were not seen again for several months. After the horses were gathered in the spring and brought to the ranch, the herd would be much different from the one that was turned out in the fall. Going through during the winter months, outlaws would exchange mounts, and leave different horses bearing brands registered all the way from Canada to Mexico. In addition, sometimes horse thieves would raid these winter ranges and get away with a good share of the saddle horse remuda.

When Fred Sharp was about twenty years old, this group of self-styled "do-good bad men," who ran the Carlisle ranch, sent him to Kansas City with a trainload of stolen cattle. To avoid any conflicting stories, Fred was the only person who went with the cattle. Somehow, word got around about the stolen cattle, and the Pinkerton Men and railroad detectives were there to intercept the train. Arrested on the spot, Fred was taken to a hotel room under guard and relentlessly questioned for three days about the stolen cattle, and about whom he was working for. Even though Fred didn't consider himself a part of the hard-case bunch that had sent him with the cattle, he remained steadfast and loyal and would not tell the authorities anything, not even his name. Very shortly the cattle brands were checked out and the owners notified by telegraph that "their cattle were being held in the Kansas City Stockyards . . . please advise." Most of the cattlemen sent power of attorney to Fred Sharp to sell their cattle and bring the check home to them.

These were hard times and hard people; some of the big outfits that had control of the range were very tough on the little guy. Their manner of operating and their attitude towards the other ranchers simply had to be "might makes right."

When Fred arrived at the Club Ranch, he was introduced to another man who had an enviable reputation with the wild ones. His name was Joe Landers, and he was from the Dragoon Mountains of southern Arizona. Like Fred Sharp, Landers was raised, almost from childhood, to chase wild cattle. Graham Mountain near Safford and the Dragoon mountains north of Tombstone were full of wild cattle around the year 1900. Joe Landers came to Colorado as a result of a band of horses that were stolen from a big cattle outfit on the Uncompaghre Plateau. Belonging to a man by the name of Hutchins, better known as "Salida Hutch," the herd of horses was tracked to a point where "Hutch" felt certain that the thieves were heading for Arizona. "Hutch" telegraphed ahead giving the Arizona sheriff a description of the horses and the brands that they wore; later, the horsethieves were picked up about fifty miles north of Douglas, Arizona. Although mighty leg-weary and sore-footed from the fast trip from Colorado, the herd was retrieved intact and in good shape. Salida Hutch wanted the horses returned to Colorado as soon as possible and gave the sheriff instructions about shipping them back. The sheriff was instructed to hire a dependable man to deliver the horses back to their home range. The man that the sheriff hired was Joe Landers.

Upon returning the horses to the Uncompaghre range, Landers decided to stick around the country for a time and look over the cattle outfits. It was common for cowboys from Arizona or New Mexico or Texas to work their way north with trail herds and then stay on in the northern country. Often, a cowman wanting to stock his range and get a quick start in the cattle business would buy an entire trail herd and hire any cowboys interested in staying on.

Around 1885, there were several million head of cattle running on the prairie country of eastern Colorado; ninety percent of them had come up the trail from Texas or New Mexico. Most of the cattle that stocked the Club range came into the country this way. Sometimes they were bought a thousand head at a time.

Now, Alex Calhoun knew that he had an ace in the hole in the person of Fred Sharp. Since he had also hired Joe Landers to work for him, he was confident that they would clean up the Club range of wild cattle.

For the first few weeks the two men just rode around getting to know the lay of the land and the hideouts for most of the wild cattle. They observed their routes for going to and from watering holes and the range areas that they were most likely to graze. For the later task of placing traps for catching the big end of the wild cattle, this observation process was critical. There would be a need for many first-class saddle horses as well. Rugged and eroded, the terrain was heavily timbered by pinon and scrub cedar on the north slopes and grass and brush on the open and south slopes. The horses that could carry men at full speed during the chasing of the wild cattle would have to be young, strong, well broken, and filled with an inborn, natural love of the chase. They would have to be good right from the start. Because there would be cattle that couldn't be trapped and would have to be run down and roped, the horses for this work would have to be trained to follow a cow anywhere she went and at whatever speed she decided to travel. The pursuit would be through thick timber and brush, and the horse would have to be broke to a *snaffel** bit, so the rider could ride the rein and let the horse carry him through the thick limbs and brushy places. All race horses are ridden with a snaffel bit; the jockey holds on by riding the rein and letting the horse pull against the bit. Many messages are transmitted from rider to horse via the reins.

A man by the name of Horace Joseph, who lived in Norwood, raised and broke some of the finest horses in the area. These horses were just exactly the type desired by Calhoun for his cowboys. Calhoun wasn't the kind of man to go short on anything, especially if a real need existed. His cowboys needed good horses, and Joseph's horses were the best around.

There was a fine quarter horse stallion in the area at this time that was a descendent of the famous stallion, Steeldust. This stallion was the sire of the string of Joseph horses that Calhoun liked so well. Because these animals had speed, endurance, intelligence and natural ability, there was a great demand for Steeldust colts from cowboys all over the country. The demand for them was not lessened by the cowboys who would be gathering wild cattle on the Club range.

Fred Sharp claimed the best horse he ever used for catching wild cattle was a spoiled race horse that he had bought from Al

* A snaffel bit is a jointed, gentler bit than a curb bit. When pulled on by the reins, the curb bit puts pressure on the bars, which is a tender portion of the horse's jaw bone behind the bridle teeth. This causes a horse to stop immediately because of the pain inflicted. A snaffel bit doesn't pull down on the bars, rather, it pulls back on the horse's mouth without causing any pain.

Fred Sharp in the "twilight of his years." (Courtesy of Mr. and Mrs. Alvin Satley.)

Neale of Norwood. Al eventually sold the horse because he got into a bad habit of bucking off his jockeys. This horse was a thoroughbred and had more endurance than the day was long. It seemed he just couldn't be worked hard enough. Even a wild mule running loose on the Club range was a cinch for this horse to run down. Allowing Fred to rope him and bring him on into the ranch, he flat ran that mule into the ground. Upon returning to the ranch the same day and hearing about Fred running down the wild mule, Joe Landers remarked that about all he was able to do that day was "rope a full grown mountain lion." After a short time, Fred took the buck out of this great animal, and he became a top-notch horse for catching wild cattle.

In addition to obtaining the best saddle horses, many cattle traps were built as well. A structure of dead trees and brush was erected around a watering place; when cattle came to drink, a man waiting at a concealed gate would close them in. Roping the cattle and hobbling them so they could only travel in a walk, the cowboys slowly drove them down to the ranch. At some earlier point, most of the cattle that had gone wild had been broken to drive by cowboys. Now, when these hobbled cattle discovered they could not get away, they settled in easily to being driven and went along rather peaceably. This was how practically all of the wild cattle were gathered. However, the mavericks and the really honest-to-goodness renegades did have to be roped and led to the ranch.

A trap in Johnson Basin netted 150 head in one drive. The trap was built at the end of a narrow gorge with high perpendicular walls. Once the cattle were spooked out of higher country into the gorge, the lower end was closed off, and the trap was made. Because the cattle could only be driven in a group of about a dozen at a time, this bunch took about two weeks to drive to the ranch after being gathered in the trap.

I'm told that some of the most breathtaking, audacious riding ever witnessed was that of Fred Sharp chasing a lone maverick in the rough country. His horse was trained to stay right on the heels of the cow critter no matter where it went, and Fred trained himself to hold on and duck the tree limbs and branches that flew by fast and thick. Fred was a small man by size, and his ability to maneuver was enhanced by this as well as by his unique leather jacket on which he had sewn two thicknesses of tough cow hide over the shoulders and back. With this much protection he could duck his head, speed through the thickest of the limbs and branches and not feel a thing. Sometimes breaking off limbs as big as a man's arm, the horse with the snaffel bit would pull him on through. No matter how thick they were, Fred never turned aside for any patches of brush; his horse was trained the same. A horse can run at amazing speed with his head ducked low. Both this horse and rider knew that was about the only way to get through the tight places where the wild cattle ran. A horse that tries to go through thick brush with its head up high will get the reins fouled in the limbs every time. Oh, to have seen the sight of Fred Sharp bent low over his race horse and to have heard the sound of non-stop cracking and scraping of brush over that heavy, tattered leather jacket!

When he roped a wild cow, Fred Sharp only used about fifteen feet of lariat rope. He would build a small loop in the rope and stick it under his leg above the knee. It would stay in place because he had to grip the saddle very tightly with his legs in order to stay on the horse. As soon as the chase led them to a clearing thirty or forty yards across, Fred would grab the rope out from under his leg and whirl it once over his head and then rope the cow by one hind leg. Since the horse was always right on the heels of the animal being chased, it didn't take long to get the rope into action. By the time the animal was roped (and before the horse would have time to start slowing it down), this threesome would be into the timber on the other side of the clearing. Now, the horse and cow did not always end up on the same side of a tree. If it happened that the cow crossed on the opposite side of a tree from the horse, a sure-fire wreck was bound to happen. If that happened, the horse and rider would both be jerked sideways into the branches and dead limbs. Trying to keep his face from being dragged through the limbs, the horse would rear back, and the cow would lunge headlong, and try to get free or break the rope. The horse and rider didn't always win the contest because the cow's foot would often slip through the loop, and she would be free—sending the cowboy and horse right back onto her trail again in search of the next clearing. One episode of getting a tree between himself and a cow was usually enough for a horse to learn to turn off sideways as soon as the cowboy jerked up his slack.

Following the chase or chases (depending on the luck of the day), Sharp went to work readying the animal for delivery to the ranch as soon as the cow critter was roped and stopped. He would use the horse to jerk the cow down, then the horse would back up on the rope holding the cow in that position while Fred sidelined* the cow with a short piece of rope. Once sidelined, a cow can get up and walk slowly but is incapable of running without continually falling down. After a few failed attempts at running, most cattle are content to walk.

If there were no more cattle around to be gathered, the next step would be to saw the tips off the horns with a small dehorning saw. All of the wild cattle had horns if they were born wild, but the branded cattle who had joined up with the original wild ones may have been dehorned as calves.

Fred remarked to me many times about the amazing old age that some of the wild cattle had lived to. The Club brand hadn't been used on range cattle since 1884, but when he started bringing in the wild ones in 1906, there were plenty of old cows still packing the Club marking. This would put their age at around twenty-two years old. It wasn't at all uncommon to find five generations of a cow's own kin running with her; sometimes the last three were still sucking. A few of the cattle were so wild that they never showed themselves in daylight hours, and their presence was known only because of the signs and tracks around. After scouting the area and locating the watering place, Sharp and Landers would wait for a bright moonlit night and then ambush the cattle when they would trail in to drink. This method was termed "moonlighting" and was much riskier to horse and rider than the daylight chases.

Fred's skill at roping and sidelining a wild cow enabled

---

* Sidelining a cow is tying the two legs on the same side together with about two or three feet of rope separating them. Cross-sidelining is tying opposite front and rear feet together.

him to catch as many as three cows in one ambush, catching up to the scattering bunch after each capture. When it came to gathering wild cattle, Fred outshone many a good ranch boss. One in particular, who thought he could outride and outrope the old jockey, galloped up to where Fred was tying down his second or third catch of this latest ambush and wondered where all of the cattle had run off to. This incident paints a very accurate picture of how far ahead of the better-than-average cowboys Fred Sharp really was.

One particular chase stands out as a dramatic example of how far Fred Sharp would go in order to catch a wild cow. One day, Fred and Joe Landers were after an especially wild cow that had eluded them many times before. She had the habit of running through almost impenetrable patches of cedar and pinon. On this certain day, the old gal was heading for heavy timber at top speed. When she reached the shelter of the trees, she didn't stop, and the chase continued as it had many times before. Fred noticed a small clearing ahead of the cow, but a huge, old cedar tree had the trail blocked off. Split by lightning, the trunk separated in halves that fell to each side. Was it possible for a man on horseback to get through and stay close enough to the cow to rope her? Fred steered his horse straight for the forked tree formed by the riven halves. With a gigantic leap, the horse cleared the tangle of branches and splintered wood. The cow had ducked under the limbs of one of the fallen halves. Before she could get straightened up to run again, Fred had his rope on one of her hind legs. Following this latest relentless pursuit, Sharp had not only earned the addition of one more wild cow on his tally card but also the inextinguishable admiration and respect of another top cowhand, Joe Landers.

Fred had some interesting ways of bringing in his day's catch. The first of the sidelined cows would be roped around the horns and held tight by the horse while Fred sawed off the tips of the horns and then removed the sideline rope. The horns were tipped so the cow couldn't hook the horse with them while being led to gather another sidelined cow. Now, a freshly caught, wild cow does not suddenly become an obedient pet that will follow at the end of a rope. The slack in the rope had to be taken up gradually until the horse and cow were side by side. Fred would then get the cow's nose up in the saddle across his leg to lead it to the next animal. With the cow's nose placed up in the saddle this way, Fred would tip the head back and cause her to lose the effectiveness of the horns. This whole process would be repeated with the next cow while the horse maintained a tight rope on both of his charges. The proper training of the cowboy's horse was paramount to the success of bringing in these cattle. With a little maneuvering, the second cow's head would be brought up across Fred's other leg. In this fashion they would make their ten or twelve mile procession to the ranch. If caught, a third cow would be left to be picked up the following day. Many times, Fred would return to the ranch in the middle of the night. Leading two head of wild cattle with their heads up across his saddle, he and his horse would step along in knightly fashion as if the steed were aware of his important role in the precarious business of snaring, collecting, and returning this clan of prodigals to the Club Ranch.

Wintertime was the most popular time to catch the wild cattle. They ranged lower in summer and higher in winter than the domestic cattle that were gathered regularly. In winter it was easy to trail them around and find their bed grounds and grazing areas. Because the frozen, icy ground didn't promote safety for the horse and rider, many violent spills were serious enough to cripple a horse permanently and put his rider in bed for a month or so. If horses did survive a bad fall, they were much better horses after that. A horse is a very intelligent animal and has a great memory when it comes to self-preservation. Through a foot of snow with ice and hidden obstacles underneath, a good horse could carry his rider in a long run, and stop a bucking, bawling old 1000–1200 pound wild cow out on the end of a catch rope at the same time. The horse had to be wary at all times and be braced for any sudden moves the cow undoubtedly would make. With a big, mean steer tied hard and fast to the saddle horn, a horse learns quickly to pay full attention and keep the upper hand when it's traveling in a bad place with treacherous footing underneath.

There were never any *dally ropers** among the men who caught wild cattle out of the breaks. Cut up by washes and ridges and usually heavily covered by scrub oak brush, these extremely rough areas served as the favorite hiding places for outlaw cattle. A popular slogan of the day summed up the circumstances of getting your rope around a wild cow rather bluntly. "If you don't want 'em, don't rope 'em." A dally roper could always let go of the rope if the situation got sticky, but tied hard and fast, a cowboy stays with whatever he catches. As described earlier, a good horse will usually keep things under control. However, chasing a wild animal at full speed, down a steep hillside where the ground is rocky and criss-crossed with small washes and ravines and fallen, dead trees, is—well, it's just asking for trouble. Still, trouble didn't deter Joe and Fred when they were on the chase. They knew their horses, and their horses knew what was expected of them. Even the best can take a fall though. When a cow, hard pressed to get away, stumbles and falls right in front of your horse, it can be a humbling experience to say the least. At times like this, the horse, cow, and cowboy would all tumble head over heels down through the

---

* Dally roping is a method of roping, whereby the opposite end from the loop is not secured to the saddle horn. When the catch is made, several wraps are taken around the saddle horn. This is called "taking dallies," from the Mexican words *da le Vuelta*: "give it a turn."

rocks and brush and wonder if perhaps there wasn't a less hazardous way to get acquainted. In the rough ole' life of a cowboy, though, it was all in a day's work. Over the next five years Joe Landers and Fred Sharp successfully whittled away at the numbers of wild cattle. In their wake, they became known in all parts as masters in their craft. Dick Blumberg, a well-respected, big cattleman on Uncompaghre considered Joe Landers the finest cowboy he had ever laid eyes on.

The price of cattle at the time Fred and Joe were bringing in the last of the wild cows, was around sixteen dollars a head. A cowboy could make good money bringing in one or two cows a day. In 1911 Fred Sharp left the Club Ranch after spending five years helping to catch around 1,500 head of wild cattle. The sale of these wild cattle paid for the running expenses of the Club Ranch for five years. When Alex Calhoun put Fred Sharp and Joe Landers on his payroll, he effectively bought five years of free management at the same time. This was represented in the numbers of wild cattle caught and sold.

Fred knew of an outfit up on Uncompaghre that had a lot of wild cattle also, and he rode on up there one day to see if he could make a contract with the foreman, Bally Watkins, to catch their wild cattle. The foreman thought that Sharp was driving a little too hard of a bargain, and they were never able to get together on a deal. So, Fred left this part of Colorado at that time and went to Meeker, Colorado where he worked for some time for the K-T outfit. Most of the wild cattle that were left on the Uncompaghre died of old age back in the rough country.

Meanwhile, Joe Landers stayed on awhile longer at the Club Ranch, but the wild cattle were getting scarce. Farther down the Dolores River there was yet another cow outfit that had plenty of wild cattle on their range. This spread was owned by John Pace, who had range clear to the Colorado River (at this time it was known as the Grand River). Since Pace had range in between the rivers, his cowboys frequently swam their horses from one side to the other when business with the cattle made it necessary. When he turned up missing in the spring of 1912, Joe Landers was thought to have drowned in the Dolores River. His horse was later found along the river quite close to a bridge that spanned it. It hardly seemed likely that he would have tried to swim the river when there was a bridge so close by. If he had tried to swim the ice-choked river that spring, the chances of his ever coming out alive were slim to non-existent. The ice jams in the Dolores River this particular spring were so bad that at the little town of Bedrock, Colorado, ice blocked the river in numerous places and caused the water to inundate all the ranch land owned by the Galloway Brothers. Even in the warm Bedrock climate, the concentration of ice in the orchard there was so great that it was June before it all melted.

When Joe Lander's sister, who lived in Arizona at that time, was notified of his presumed death, she came to the area where Joe had been working. It is not known whether she came to identify his body or not. What is known is that she stayed around a few months in the hopes that when the high water receded Joe's body would be found. It never was. She returned to Arizona with no proof one way or the other of Joe's fate. Today, Joe's disappearance is still considered an unsolved mystery.

At about this same time, tragedy struck another of the former Club Ranch cowboys. His name was Ben Lowe, a Delta, Colorado native who was very well-liked by the people who knew him. Sometime after Ben left the Club Ranch, a miscarriage of justice forced him into the life of an outlaw. One day, Lowe and his two sons were riding in Escalante Canyon when they met up with Cash Sampson, the ex-Sheriff of Delta County. Lowe told his sons that he wanted to talk with Sampson for a while and sent them down the trail a ways to wait for him. He said he would catch up with them shortly; it was a rendezvous he never made.

Lowe and Sampson shot it out to the death that day in Escalante, and their bodies were later found just a few feet apart by Lowe's two sons.

In 1913, Calhoun bought out his partner, Selby, and continued to run the Club Ranch until 1915 when he sold it to the partnership of Butterfield and Christie. This partnership held the Ranch until about 1920 when it was sold again (this time to a man by the name of Hamby). Hamby only operated the ranch for a couple of years and sold it to a prominent Norwood stockman, Mr. Ed Lavender in 1922. Lavendar had been in the banking business with a partner named Wheeler. When Ed bought the Club Ranch, Wheeler took over the banking business; Ed went strictly into cattle ranching. When Ed acquired it, the Club range had no cattle, but he did have a lot of cattle up around the Lone Cone. To stock the Club range again, his cowboys trailed a bunch of them down the mountain. Lavender kept the Club Ranch until his death in the spring of 1935, at which time his entire operation went into an estate. The estate was administered by Jack Lamb, and the principal buyers were Al Herndon of Norwood, Charley Redd of La Sal, Utah and Dan Hughes Sr. of Montrose. Since the Club Ranch was pretty much out of the way of the other holdings of these three stockmen, they all declined to keep the land. Not long afterwards, all the deeded ground was bought by the United States Vanadium Corporation which later became Union Carbide Corporation.

Converting a ranch into a mining operation required a lot of heavy earth-moving equipment and the manpower to operate it. What would follow in the hustle and bustle at the construction site would change forever the face of that famous old property. When the last of the old buildings was torn down and the man in the bulldozer built a huge pond in its place, it could be said with some degree of finality that the era of the Club Ranch had finally come to a close.

INDEX